HOWELL HARRIS AND THE DAWN OF REVIVAL

A map of the part of Wales connected with the early life of Howell Harris

HOWELL HARRIS AND THE DAWN OF REVIVAL

RICHARD BENNETT

translated from the Welsh by
GOMER M. ROBERTS

EVANGELICAL PRESS OF WALES

First published in Welsh under the title *Blynyddoedd Cyntaf Methodistiaeth*
(tr. *The First Years of Methodism*), 1909.

First English edition (by the Banner of Truth Trust, under the title
The Early Life of Howell Harris), 1962.

This edition (by the Evangelical Press of Wales, with an index,
revised bibliography and new title), 1987.

Cover Picture: Cregennan Lake, near Dolgellau at sunrise (by courtesy of the
Wales Tourist Board).

Published by the Evangelical Press of Wales, Bryntirion, Bridgend,
Mid Glamorgan CF31 4DX.
Printed by Bridgend Printing Co. Ltd., Tremains Road, Bridgend.

CONTENTS

——————

PUBLISHERS' NOTE

The footnotes not ascribed to the translator or the publisher are those retained from the original Welsh edition. Many of the original footnotes referred to works in Welsh and therefore have been omitted.

NOTE TO THE 1987 EDITION

The publishers are grateful to Mr S. M. Houghton for compiling the index for this new edition.

INTRODUCTION

As the one primarily responsible for the suggestion that this book should be translated and published I am happy to write a word of introduction and recommendation.

The very fact that I have made the suggestion shows in itself the value that I attach to it. I have long felt that those who cannot read and understand the Welsh language should be given the opportunity of reaping some of the benefits and blessings that I have enjoyed from reading this book.

Let me introduce its contents.

It is not a complete biography of Howell Harris. It concentrates in great detail only upon the first three years of his spiritual history. There are two or three full biographies of him in book form (out of print alas!) and also articles on him in certain larger works on Welsh Calvinistic Methodism. But the object of Richard Bennett, the original author, was to allow us to see the working of God's Spirit in the soul of Howell Harris in the detailed manner recorded in Harris's own diaries, in these first formative and thrilling years. Bennett therefore rightly felt that his own remarks should be reduced to a minimum, and that all that was required of him was to supply the connecting links in the story so as to enable the reader to understand the various allusions to actual events. He does not attempt to comment upon, still less to apply or to enforce, what is revealed in the extracts from Harris's diaries. He was too sensitive spiritually to do so, and probably felt the ground was so holy that he could but take off the shoes from off his feet and be silent in awe. I have always been most grateful to him for this.

No! Here we have Howell Harris himself making bare his soul and allowing us to read of God's dealings with him. As spiritual autobiography it is practically unrivalled. A more honest soul than Harris never lived. That was the testimony of all his contemporaries to him. There is a sense in which he was almost too honest and too sensitive. But who are we in this decadent, super-ficial and glib age to say that?

At times we are privileged to look on at the struggles of a mighty soul and made to feel something of its agony. At other times we listen to the praises and thanksgiving of a soul virtually lifted up to the third heaven and knowing such outpourings of the Holy Spirit and work-ings of the love of God that he could scarce contain them.

Anyone who reads this book carefully will derive great spiritual benefit. He will be troubled and uplifted, cor-rected and encouraged. Some may well feel that they have never hitherto been Christians at all if this is really what is possible to the Christian. Others in self defence and resisting the Spirit, will feel that this is but "enthu-siasm" and "ecstasy," the two things that a "moderate," formal, respectable, Laodicean Christianity always abom-inates.

But read it for yourself!

Quite apart from these considerations which are the chief reason for reading it, this book is quite invaluable from the historical standpoint. Howell Harris was an intimate friend of Whitefield, the Wesleys and the other leaders of the evangelical awakening in England in the 18th century. He frequently preached for Whitefield in London and acted as his deputy while the latter was in America.

As for the history of the same revival in Wales and the origin of what is now known as the Presbyterian Church of Wales what is recorded here is crucial and essential.

Ryle in his work, *The Christian Leaders of the Last Century*, did not include Harris because he never became an ordained clergyman. The reasons for that are explained here and are of fascinating interest in and of themselves.

Nothing is more profitable, after the reading of the Bible itself and books that help us to understand it, than the reading of the biography or autobiography of a great Christian man. Howell Harris was a great man and a genius in a natural sense, a brilliant organiser and improvisor—a man who would have succeeded in almost any walk in life. He had a complex and fascinating personality which made him inevitably a prince and a leader amongst men. He takes his place naturally and as an equal in the distinguished company to which I have already referred.

He was not as great a preacher as Daniel Rowland and George Whitefield, but as an exhorter he was probably superior to both. But what amazes us and humbles us and condemns us is his humility and his utter submission to our Lord at all costs. This is why God used him in such a mighty manner.

Would you know something of what is meant by the term "revival"? Would you know the real meaning of, "the Spirit itself beareth witness with our spirit that we are the children of God"? Would you know more of "life in the Spirit," and "prayer in the Spirit," and something of "the powers of the world to come"? Then read this book and remember that Howell Harris was but "a man of like passions with ourselves" and that Jesus Christ is "the same yesterday, today and forever."

The translation is faithful and clear. I pray that this

book may be so blessed and used as to cause many to cry out saying, "where is the Lord God of Howell Harris?"

D. MARTYN LLOYD-JONES,

Westminster Chapel,
London.

HIS YOUTH

On 15 February 1733 the Rev. Griffith Jones of Llanddowror wrote as follows to his friend, Mrs. Bridget Bevan of Laugharne:

> . . . If we consider how numerous and shameless, I may say, how common and impudent the despisers and opposers of serious piety are in our days, what shall we think but that the enemy is coming in like a water-flood, and threatens to overflow our land with a worse deluge than that which drowned the world in the days of Noah. And though for any thing I know, it may be suffered to proceed to a greater extremity, than we have yet seen, yet in God's due time, I trust he will seasonably and surprisingly lift up a standard against the enemies and persecutors of Jesus Christ; . . . Reasons and human means only, will not serve to stop the tide of iniquity, which now flows so fast upon us. No standard will suffice to oppose it but that of the Holy Spirit's lifting up.

On 11 March 1735 he wrote again to the same lady:

> . . . Our neglect of religion, especially the spiritual part of it, has caused our sins to increase to a vast height; and it is evident, that we ripen very fast for some terrible judgment, which we must expect to feel soon, if God in infinite mercy prevents it not by sending a double portion of a reforming spirit among us.

Griffith Jones's confidence was soon justified. Even when he was writing of the necessity of "a double portion of a reforming spirit," during that very month the word of the Lord came to Howell Harris, a young man from Breconshire, and it did not cease to work in him until he was made a special messenger of Heaven to his age and nation.

As to his circumstances, he was of the common people. No long pedigree could be drawn up for him, connecting him with a rich and noble ancestry. About the year 1700 a carpenter from Carmarthenshire came to live in the district of Talgarth in Breconshire. His name was Howell Powell, or Harris. His sole capital, as far as we know, was a certificate declaring that the parish of Llangadog would support him if ever he needed parochial charity in his new home. In 1702 he married a young girl named Susannah Powell and they lived among her people in the hamlet of Trevecka, near Talgarth. There, in the carpenter's cottage, the children were born —Joseph, Anne, Thomas, and the youngest, who was born in January 1714, and was named after his father, Howell Harris.

It seems that his parents walked circumspectly, and they used to attend the public service in their parish church, together with their children. We have reason to think, too, that they did not fully neglect another important duty—religious instruction in their home. The youngest child vividly remembered himself as a boy of seven walking to Talgarth church with his brother to recite his catechism. He experienced profound impressions at times at that tender age. God's greatness and the importance of eternity pressed so heavily on his mind that if he saw the village children playing on the Sabbath he could not refrain from rebuking them.

His first teacher and his best friend was his brother Joseph; but he soon lost him. Joseph was a blacksmith, but he soon showed that he was no ordinary man. We do not know what prowess he showed before he left home, but we know that somehow he drew attention to himself and that he was as inexplicable to his fellows and as insane in their sight as his youngest brother afterwards became. He was a taciturn man, always keeping his sorrow and his joy to himself and burying himself in study and scientific experiments. But between the joints of this armour an arrow reached his heart. In a mansion the other side of the valley there lived a young lady of about his own age. He fell in love with her in spite of the difference in their stations, and one day he ventured to reveal to her the state of his feelings. The young lady was furious and commanded him not to think of her and not to utter a word to her ever again. The blow was too severe. He determined to leave home, and sought to assuage his sorrow by going away as far from her as he possibly could. He was in London for many years, winning for himself a good position, and publishing a book on some branch of his favourite study; but his sorrow was not mitigated. Once and again he visited the West Indies for many months, but in spite of his travels and many vicissitudes, the maid of Tredwstan was in his thoughts wherever he went. After spending a period of his life in this miserable condition, he at last divulged the cause of his discontent to his brother. Howell took upon himself the task of interceding with the lady on his brother's behalf, and before long they were united together in marriage. We understand that some of their descendants have an honoured place to this day among the Breconshire gentry.[1]

In all his joys and sorrows Joseph Harris kept up his

[1] Joseph Harris (1704-64) went to London in 1724, and became friendly with Halley, the royal astronomer. He visited the West Indies in 1725 and 1730-2 to test certain nautical instruments. In 1737 he became the assistant assay-master of the King's Mint (which gave him the right to reside at the Tower of London); he was appointed the chief assay-master in 1748. His first book, *The Description and Uses of the Celestial Globe and Orrery*, was published in 1729, and three other scientific works of his were subsequently published. His wife was Anne, the daughter and co-heiress of Thomas Jones, Esq., of Tredwstan, near Trevecka.—G. M. R.

interest in his relatives in Wales and cared for them. As Eliakim, the son of Hilkiah of old, he was the counsellor and defender of his father's house in all difficulties. But Howell, the youngest of the family, was his Benjamin, his dear one. He urged his parents to give him a better education than was usual in those days, and persuaded them from time to time not to be disheartened by their straitened circumstances. In 1725 he wrote to his parents saying how glad he was to hear of their design to send Howell to school, promising them every help within his power. This was an elementary school, kept probably in one of the local churches.[1] But in 1728 he was placed in a grammar school kept at Llwyn-llwyd in the parish of Llanigon near Hay.

At Llwyn-llwyd Harris studied the rudiments of Greek and Latin and mastered them to some extent. He uses a good deal of Latin in his earlier diaries. He used to say in later years that he was then conversant with history, politics, games, and much else that would make him an interesting companion to rich and poor alike. With such a vivacious and animated nature he could not be very moderate in anything he took in hand. He threw himself into all the amusements and innocent mischief of his fellow-students. We can scarcely believe that he went far astray while he was there, though there are some statements in the diaries which suggest it. He was dangerously ill during the end of the summer of 1729, and doubtless this checked him somewhat.

He had not yet chosen his calling, but his brother, in August 1730, pressed upon him to do so in order to give a more definite trend to his studies. It seems that he thought of the ministry of the Church at that time. In

---

[1] The Latin diaries show that during his boyhood Howell Harris attended schools at Talgarth and at Llanfihangel Tal-y-llyn.—G. M. R.

October 1730 Joseph sailed for the second time to
Jamaica, and before setting out he wrote home to this
effect:

> I would not have my Brother be in the least disconsolate
> at my departure. I go upon a Sure footing, and I Shall
> have it at heart to See him in a way of getting his lively-
> hood, to do which no endeavours of mine Shall be want-
> ing. I reckon he is Now almost gone thro' the Grammar
> School, and if ever he Should be a Clergyman it is not so
> very material whether he has had an University Educa-
> tion. Let him mind his Classicks and take care not to for-
> get what he has already learnt; the Latin and Greek
> Tongues will be a key to him to read other Books which
> hereafter he may have occasion for. I would have him
> also endeavour to inform himself in writing, and then
> he'll have another String to his Bow. I wish he Could get
> a School or Some Such thing to Employ him in the
> Countrey till I return, and I hope you'll do your End-
> eavours to keep him from any Servile Employment for
> that Time.

But a greater loss than the departure of his brother was
near. In March 1731 his father died. Thus, Howell
was obliged to leave Llwyn-llwyd at the end of the term
and go out to seek for some means of earning his living.

In January 1732 he was appointed schoolmaster at
Llan-gors, a small township near Syfaddan Lake, not far
from his home. He was there for eighteen months at
least—possibly a few months longer. His mother was
anxious on his account, predicting adversity; for Llan-
gors bore a doubtful reputation in those days. He himself, by then, was a youth of eighteen, without much to
occupy him, with no father to rule him and no brother
at hand to give him advice. Thus he was given a free
rein at a dangerous period of his life, and it is sad to
relate that he rapidly went down hill. He spent his
leisure in the counsel of the ungodly and in the seat of

the scornful.   He neglected his classics, reading plays and
such vanities.   He was the soul of every company, and
the source of fun in all the exploits and games of the
locality.   He was ready to debate on every question, and
he delighted in mocking the few Nonconformists in the
neighbourhood.   The memory of Llan-gors was sore to
him throughout his life, "the place where I first broke
out in the devil's service."   "Many of you used to go
with me towards hell," he once said while preaching
there, "and God's grace must have been free, or else I
would not have received it, because I was the worst of
you all."   And the saddest part of the story is that no
one tried to check him in his course, not even the Nonconformists, "They were very ready to debate with me
concerning outward things," he said, "but no one told
me that I was on the way to hell."

Yet he could not find peace of spirit in this way.   An
occasional sermon would give him a distaste for frivolity,
awakening memories and creating a yearning for better
things.   He once dreamed that the great Day of Judgment had arrived, and that he was standing before the
judgment-seat and compelled to give an account of himself.   These things drove him to vow to mend his ways,
and even to attempt praying.   "I tried to turn to God in
my own power, but I did not succeed until the day of
His power came."   And this, at length, was drawing nigh.

During his stay at Llan-gors his brother returned from
Jamaica and he visited his relatives in Wales.   He was
so pleased with his young brother that he revealed to
him the secret concerning Miss Anne Jones.   It seems,
however, that Howell was unsatisfied with his position
in life, for we find Joseph advising him to resign himself
for a while, promising to look for something better for
him as soon as he could.   Joseph wrote to his brother in
August 1732:

I hope you'll always remember what past betwixt us at Bristol, and keep entirely to yourself the Secret I entrusted you with. You may believe I Shall always be glad to hear whatever you can inform me from that quarter . . . it is with pleasure I Say that your behaviour and Character I had of you in the Countrey, adds to the opinion I had of you. You know how to behave always humble and affable; That, with a Sincerity and Care in discharging the trust you take upon you, will always gain you the good will of every body.

Joseph was as good as his word. A friend of his lived in Oxford, one Mr. W. Harte, the vice-principal of St. Margaret Hall. Through his good offices, he found a remunerative appointment for Howell, in Hampshire, as a schoolmaster. In November 1734 he writes to him concerning the place. "I hope the thing will be worth your Acceptance for the present, especially as you'll have an Opportunity of taking a degree at Oxford as well as if you was to Serve your time there." By this time Howell had left Llan-gors, and was in charge of a school on the other side of the lake, in the old church of Llangasty [Tal-y-llyn]. He lodged with a gentleman named Mr. Lewis Jones, of Trebinsiwn Mansion in that parish; Mr. Jones's children were with him at school—Lewis taking well to his Latin, and Billy wholly otherwise. As a rule Howell spent his week-ends at his mother's home, attending the Sunday services fairly regularly at Talgarth church. But although he was now twenty-one years of age, and his mind set upon the ministry for years, he had never yet approached the Lord's Table. It is quite possible that the cause of this was complete indifference; but it is equally possible that a measure of tenderness in his conscience kept him from trifling with the most sacred things while following such a loose life.

Some difficulty or other kept on recurring with regard

to the school in Hampshire, so that Harris was at Llan-gasty until November 1735. He tells us time and again that he himself had no hand in the cause of this confusion, but before long he came to see the finger of God in it all, for the "great turning-point" in his life was now at hand, through which the insignificant schoolmaster of Llangasty became, not a school teacher in England, but the Apostle of Jesus Christ to the Welsh people, who at that time were in a condition of utter spiritual destitution.

HIS CONVERSION

As it has already been said, religion had sunk to a very low level in the Established Church at that time. But the Lord had left to the Church "a handful of corn." "Yet gleaning-grapes shall be left in it, as the shaking of an olive-tree, two or three berries in the top of the uppermost bough, four or five in the outmost fruitful branches thereof."[1] We shall have occasion to refer to some of them later on. The majority of the clergy were content to leave their parishioners to live just as they pleased. They did not care for anything except collecting their tithes and enjoying their own corrupt pleasures. Mercifully, there was found among these churchmen another class, men who were relatively cultured and moral. These men had a higher view of the responsibility of their office, and attempted to fulfil their duties. They saw to it that the prescribed services were held regularly in their churches. They supported the English schools of the S.P.C.K. and the efforts of the Society for the Reformation of Manners. Behind their labour, no doubt, there was some desire to promote the good of the people, but little success—if any—followed their efforts. This is not surprising, because the Doctrine of Grace had vanished from the pulpits. For the most part, they preached a dry morality, so that neither they nor their hearers felt much authority or life-giving power in the ministry. As a result they placed all the emphasis on outward authority,[2] bitterly opposing all who, in their view, lacked it. It was from these men who, like Saul

[1] Isa. xvii. 6.   [2] By this they meant ordination.—Pub.

of Tarsus of old, were more highly gifted and irreproach-
able in their conduct than the majority of their brethren,
that Nonconformity and Methodism received the most
stubborn and resolute opposition.

The Rev. Pryce Davies, the vicar of Talgarth, was one
of this class. Having said that he gave much of his time
to the following of hounds and that at times he was guilty
of over-indulgence in strong drink, with the result that
he tended to forget that the servant of the Lord should
not strive, we have said the worst about him. He did his
work with much faithfulness. His church would never
be found closed nor his pulpit vacant on Sundays, and
services would be held there on week-days too. When he
was raised to the magisterial bench, he probably imitated
the rest of his brethren by aiming to do from that place
what he could not perform through the pulpit alone.
But in spite of the law, and some sort of gospel, no sign
of reformation was to be seen. Few came to hear the
Word, and fewer still came to the Lord's Table. The
Sunday before Easter in the spring of 1735, Mr. Davies
preached on the necessity of partaking of the Holy Communion, and among other things he made the following
remark: "You say that you are not fit to come to the
Table. Well, then, I say that you are not fit to pray;
yea, you are not fit to live and neither are you fit to
die."

The young schoolmaster of Llangasty had come to the
service that morning quite unconcerned, as usual. But
the vicar's remark pierced through all his indifference
and reached his heart like a sword-thrust. He there and
then determined to come to the Table on the following
Sunday. On the way home he met one of his best friends,
Joseph Saunders, a smith in the hamlet of Trevecka, and
he repeated the vicar's words to him in such solemn and
earnest tones that their echo was in the smith's ears for

a long time; and they were eventually blessed as the means of his conversion. Further on he met another villager, Evan the Weaver. Although they were at enmity, yet, in obedience to the injunction read at the end of the sermon, he approached him, and, admitting his fault, begged his forgiveness, and the two became reconciled. This was the first time for Harris to act in opposition to the low inclinations of his own nature. This serious-mindedness persisted to some degree throughout the week. In the chancel the following Sunday, the impression was deepened by the thought that he had come unworthily to the Lord's Table. He saw that it was not enough to attend Holy Communion, and he resolved to follow a new life from that hour. We do not know how far he clung to his resolution, but we do know that the impression made upon his mind gradually weakened. Only a fear of turning back and losing something prevented him from reverting to his old habits.

At last, the fourth Sunday—20 April 1735—drew near, an ever-memorable day in the history of Howell Harris. For some reason he did not return to his home that week-end, according to his custom, but he stayed at his lodging at Trebinsiwn Mansion. About nine o'clock on Sunday morning, when the resolutions and impressions of the previous three weeks were well-nigh blotted out and forgotten, he picked up as it were accidentally an old book, *The Whole Duty of Man*. He turned the pages to and fro without purpose, until at last his eyes were fixed on a particular page. He began to read the headings on self-examination, and suddenly a light above the brightness of the sun flashed upon his mind, so that he knew himself for the first time a lost and ruined sinner.

"All my natural faculties were confounded in the

shock." The fear of turning back now became terribly strong—for in that way lay damnation. But the light he had received so far, cast but little light on the future; it showed up the danger without pointing out the deliverance from it. He thus groped in the darkness seeking relief. He knew nothing himself of the way of salvation; and since he had no one to guide him, it is no wonder that he went astray. He began to work his way towards freedom under the testament that begets bondage. He returned to Trevecka on Friday evening, and on Saturday he told Joseph Saunders of the light he had received on his condition, and his resolve to fight his way towards life. He found in the smith a man ready and eager to join him. The first task they took in hand was an endeavour to keep the Sabbath. They arose early next morning and kept away from the villagers all day so as not to be tempted to speak of worldly things; and they stayed out late before retiring to sleep. On the first Sunday in May, four Trevecka people endeavoured to keep the Sabbath, and five the following Sunday.

Harris spent these weeks in reading, prayer and fasting, striving against sin. He renounced everything—all his pleasures, all his friends, rich and poor (he states that he was then acquainted with some of the leading people of the county); his fine clothes, which he had once prized so much; and every thought of worldly promotion. He lived on bread and water; he fasted for a day, then for two days, and before long for three days every week; he repaid everybody he had occasioned any loss, as far as he could remember; and he shared the little money he had left among the poor. He feared in his heart to utter a single word on the Sabbath lest he should pollute the day; and he considered it nothing to retrace his steps a long distance if he could not remember for certain whether he had closed gates, etc. After living for some time like a hermit, in a manner wholly different from his former practice, his sense of restlessness began to quieten again. He felt that at last he really was fleeing from all evil, and following all that was good. He became sufficiently confident to challenge his conscience to convict him of anything, if it could. If anyone would be saved, he was the man, for he had done his best. The only danger was backsliding; and in order to use every diligence to avoid this he spent all his leisure in secret prayer.

But this was a short and treacherous lull. Shortly the storm renewed itself; his confidence was but a spider's web. About this time, if I am not mistaken, he went to Talgarth church one Sunday fairly confident in his mind. A young man named Badham was preaching there, and his subject was the necessity of growing in grace. This threw Harris into terrible perplexity once more, because it was all he could do to keep himself from backsliding, not to mention any progress! About the same time he read in a book that he who had led others astray should do his utmost to bring them back again to the right way; as otherwise he would be held responsible for them. Behold, another burden laid upon him, utterly overwhelming him! Formerly he longed to escape from the world's turmoil and fly away to the solitude of the wilderness, so that he might not fall away. But he dared not look that way any more, with the bloodhounds at his heels. He began to exhort a little, first of all to his mother, then to Joseph and Evan, to his uncle and aunt next door, and the two John Prossers, etc. But his mind became more and more disturbed. He became conscious of some inner voice whispering to him, "Since there is no God, why bother? Are you not free? Throw away every yoke, and take your own way." He never knew before the strength of the enemy's assaults, as he had always given

way to them.   He became now, at times, almost a terror
to himself.

One day, about the middle of May, he retired to pray
in the belfry of Llangasty church.   There, in his agony,
he felt a strong urge coming upon his spirit to give himself to God.   He had never before heard of such a thing,
and he had no idea how to do so, or why.   The tempter
warned him to be wary—he would not have his own way
any longer if he did so.   But the strange compulsion pro-
duced a strong persuasion in his mind, quite different
from anything he had experienced before.   It did not
terrorise him as his former fears had done, neither did
it compel him as a brute beast, but so irresistibly did it
influence him that he was made perfectly willing to give
himself absolutely to the Lord.

Though his burden had become somewhat lighter
after "the great struggle," as he calls it, he had not yet
received a testimony that God would accept him.   Besides, what if God, after all, did not exist?   The strong
man armed had seen the danger of losing his goods.   The
temptation to Atheism returned ten times stronger than
before.   He had given himself to a God he did not yet
know, with the result that he knew not what to hold on
to, at the approach of the enemy.   Sometimes, when the
sky was clear, he would write on a piece of paper, "I
believe and I know that God exists."   Then, when the
assault came, he would run to his paper for deliverance.
But the devil made short work of the paper.   In this state
of confusion he came to realise little by little not only
his own sinfulness but to some extent his inability to save
himself.

It seems that his chief guide at this juncture was the
book, *The Practice of Piety*.   He read there that deliverance from all temptations that assail mankind could be
found in the Sacrament, provided one went to it believ-

ing that was so. And that forgiveness for every sin, confessed and acknowledged, could be had in the same place if one had faith to believe this. (This is the first glimpse given to him of the place of faith in his salvation.) His hopes revived at this, as Whitsunday and the Sacrament were at hand. He came home from Llangasty on the preceding Wednesday; and on the Thursday morning, on his knees, he began to write a list of his known sins since the age of four, in order that he might confess them before God so as to obtain pardon. He continued at it until Saturday evening, fasting during the whole time.

On Whitsunday morning, in obedience to the exhortations and warnings of their young neighbour, the majority of the villagers wended their way to church, he himself among them. The story of that service is to be found here and there throughout the diaries. "After being in hell for five weeks, I came to church fully expecting that I should lose my burden. About twelve o'clock, at the end of the sermon, the temptation fell upon me more fiercely than ever. Satan roared dreadfully within me, so that I could almost have shouted out, 'There is no God.' He had but a short season to reign, and he rent me in unspeakable fashion, breathing into my heart the most blasphemous thoughts—that I was above God, and tempting me to laugh at Him. I was wholly passive, without power to do anything, or to bring any argument to defend myself; that was just as well, otherwise I should have been fighting Satan with his own weapons, and should have been overcome. I simply said, 'If there is no God, how was the Communion ever invented, and why are so many wise people deceived?' But immediately before the Sacrament, the One who is stronger came in (after I had found power to open the door to Him a few days previously, when I was made willing); and if Satan was not then cast out, I know not when he went. At the Table, Christ bleeding on the cross was kept before my eyes constantly; and strength was given me to believe that I was receiving pardon on account of that blood. I lost my burden: I went home leaping for joy; and I said to a neighbour who was sad, 'Why are you sad? I know my sins have been forgiven,' though I had not heard that such a thing was to be found, except in this book [*The Practice of Piety*]. Oh, blessed day! would that I might remember it gratefully evermore."

He began to live a new life from that day onward. He completely lost the anxiety for his own happiness, together with every fear of falling away. A view of the great Pardoner's love towards him quickened love in his own soul, which could not be satisfied until it showed itself in acts of obedience and devotion to its Object. On Monday, forgetting his weakness, he resolved not to sin any more, but to live entirely to the Lord. He adopted the directions of *The Practice of Piety* and *The Whole Duty of Man* to regulate his life; and in order to keep a closer watch on himself than ever before, he began to keep a diary. In the beginning this was to be something between himself and God alone. He recorded everything in it—his most secret thoughts, every whim that flitted through his heart, and even his dreams. At first he could do so without giving any offence to the reader, because his soul was dancing ecstatically in the warmth of his first love. And in a fortnight or three weeks that love burst forth into a blazing fire, consuming his whole nature.

Doubtless, the experience of forgiveness in Talgarth church was sweet. Yet it left a feeling of further need in his soul which he could not define. But when he was at secret prayer in Llangasty church, the sacred spot where he had given himself to God, God now gave Himself to him:

> *There his earnest prayer was answered,*
> *There was heard his urgent plea,*
> *And his hungry soul was sated*
> *By Jehovah One in Three.*

The richest biblical terms are heaped one on another in an attempt to give expression to his experience at that time. He was there cleansed from all his idols, and the love of God was shed abroad in his heart. Christ had come in previously, but now He began to sup with him; now he received the Spirit of adoption, teaching him to cry Abba Father, and with it a desire to depart and be with Christ. All his *fears* vanished for months, and pure love took their place.

Immediately after this he was annoyed by one of his pupils and he "felt some risings of anger" in his heart. Instantly the devil asserted in his face, "You have fallen from grace, and forfeited all your treasure." For a moment he was staggered. He was strongly tempted to commit suicide, but mercifully he was restrained from so doing. In the fury of the storm the words, "I, the Lord, change not," shot into his mind with such power that the turbulent sea within him was quieted. He had never heard before of this word of Scripture, but to his dying day he loved it more than any other word. In the darkest periods, when every star was obscured and all hope had vanished, his soul clung to this verse. This was his sure anchor, and it kept its hold a thousand times after all else had given way. This verse brought him to "the glorious liberty of the children of God" and to realise that what alone mattered was God's "mighty grasp of him." That is why we find in the diary the words, "The work was finished about June."

THE FIRST SUMMER
(June-November 1735)

As the early diaries are written in Latin, we must gather the story of these first months from the later diaries.[1] This is a disadvantage; because the same things appear in different aspects to Harris in various periods of his life. He does not relate the story of an incident in his inner life in the same form in 1736 as he does in 1738 or 1740. At the beginning he was in a sense somewhat ignorant. He went through the great changes noted in the last chapter in almost complete ignorance of the terms that would commonly be used to describe them. Although he had experience of these things, he could not always relate them in an orderly and consistent manner to others. When he began to think of matters theologically, he was a rank Arminian. But about 1737 he embraced Calvinism—and henceforward all accounts of his early history are coloured by that system. Whenever he received a fuller revelation of some truth, that would fill his mind for a season, and he would view everything in the light of it. The first heaven and the first earth would not be remembered, and no thought would be given to them. After some years he saw in a new light the work of the Second Person of the Trinity in his salvation, and after that there are many statements in the diary to the effect that he knew nothing of Christ until

---

[1] Harris's diaries in English and in Welsh are often almost undecipherable, owing to the small writing and the use of abbreviations. When he used Latin the problem of deciphering becomes well-nigh impossible. Hence this remark.—Pub.

1738. Similarly he says that he knew nothing of faith, nor
of the work of the Holy Spirit, until he met George
Whitefield in 1739. But in calmer moments these wild
words are withdrawn, and he thanks God for the old
mercies of Talgarth and Llangasty. The reader will per-
ceive that it is no easy task to weave one consistent story
from these seeming inconsistencies.

These months again were spent in Llangasty, and he
greatly loved the loneliness and the seclusion he found
there. He read, prayed and fasted again, as before, deny-
ing himself all things in order to mortify the flesh, until
the state of his health was impaired. He knew of no
other way of pleasing God whom he loved so much.
Every book he read, every sermon he heard, tended to
engage him more and more with duty, keeping him away
from Christ. He complains bitterly that he never heard
the *Gospel* being preached during this period of his life.
Serious defects must be admitted in him, too, such as his
insufficient knowledge of the Word of God, and his un-
faithfulness to the revelation he had received directly in
his own heart during the various stages of his conversion.
His faith was strengthened somewhat by reading the
first part of *Hand's Practical Catechism*. Often after this
he would compare his faith with Abraham's, wondering
whether he could have left his country and all else, and
whether he could believe that which was seemingly impossible at the command of his Lord. He greatly revered
his unevangelical teachers, although his soul would have
starved if he had depended upon them. In some measure
he saw his danger, and in August we find him entreating
his vicar for a monthly administration of the Sacrament,
so that the heavenly spark might not be quenched.

But in spite of the low Arminianism which was thrust
into his head, his heart was at the same time filled with
the love of God. There was a great difference between

his theology and his faith. "He filled me with His love years before He taught me how He redeemed and saved me." Oftentimes he doubted his faith, and he denied it completely many times, but he never doubted his love. He walked in full assurance of this. He states that he lived on love like a child eating fruit, without knowing anything of the tree on which it grew. A constantly repeated expression in moments of exaltation in later years is, "I have not found myself so full of God since the first year." Sin fled when he looked upwards. Whenever unbelief suggested that he was unfit to be with Christ, his heart would answer at once that Christ could make him fit in a moment. "Though I knew not the meaning of grace, I knew that God loved me. The question 'who maketh thee to differ from another?' filled my mind constantly, and the realisation that He loved me above all others, in turn made me love Him too with all my heart. Were it not for the love I had tasted, I should have given up; I never could have gone against the current. Love fell in showers on my soul, so that I could scarcely contain myself. I had no fear, or any doubt of my salvation; but yet," he says, mixing his experience with his theology, "I must then have been under the law."

This love kept away from his heart every particle of love for the world. He lost every care with regard to his circumstances, and for the future. He cast himself on the bare promise of the "God that cannot lie," and he was cared for; although he was often penniless and sometimes in debt, he never lacked anything. "I received the Spirit of Christ seven years ago," he wrote in the summer of 1742, "and I never after that knew anything of the love of money, or the love of the world, although I was plagued by every other corruption. If I had ten thousand pounds a year, I would freely share all between the lambs. Oh, that I had been born in the days of the Apostles, when everything was so simple, with zeal burning and flaming."

Another effect of this love was to fill him with courage to counsel every one he met concerning their souls. Some say that his portrait shows a man courageous by nature, "made without fear." But he himself always held that he was by nature as timid as a hare, and that what courage he possessed was a gift from above, given to him directly from heaven for the sake of his work. "I felt I was all love—so full of it that I could not ask for more. I walked in the light of God's countenance, I met Him in all things; and the strength of the love I experienced enabled me to go through all oppositions that came up against me. All fears vanished, and I was as one established upon a rock, living in faith and power, having renounced all worldly things. I was supported by an unseen power, and I was comfortably and powerfully led by perpetual outpourings of love into my soul almost every time I prayed. Such a coward was I by nature, and such power the Lord gave unto me!"

It was gradually that this courage began to show itself. "In June, I began to read to some of my neighbours in my mother's house concerning the Sacrament and church attendance. Then I read in a book that it was my duty to visit the sick, and to read to them. This led me to the village of Tredwstan to see an old man, a hundred years of age, named Jenkin Laurence; and there, while I was reading to him, the neighbours gathered to listen. This made me feel much ashamed, lest I should be called a preacher, a name I hated. Afterwards I thought I ought to go and exhort all those with whom I had formerly sinned; and so I went to three villages—one on each side of our village. In this way I spent my Sunday afternoons, and would also come home during the week,

travelling by foot four miles from the place where I kept
school. I could not rest without seeing them, and
although I did not have much authority [in exhorting
them], I felt that I had to go. I shared a little money
between them until I had given all away. Oh! the
beginning was small indeed. Behold what a great bon-
fire came from a little spark! How can I show it honestly
to the coming ages, to the praise of God's glory? It was
He who began it, wholly of Himself, and from Himself
He continues to carry it on."

This small company formed a kind of "society," many
months before such a thing was heard of. In a letter
which Harris sent to Vicar Davies, requesting that they
might receive the Sacrament more frequently, he mentions that many had joined him in strict observance of
their duties, and that they had for some time sincerely
endeavoured to practice the excellent doctrines they had
received from his pulpit. And that they had vowed and
resolved, by God's help, to direct their course towards
heaven, in spite of all obstacles. This simple movement
can be looked upon as the seed of the Welsh [Calvinistic]
Methodism. But the people of Trevecka and the surrounding district proved to be unresponsive soil, and
much of the seed became unfruitful.

"Thank God for Joseph Saunders," said Harris more
than once. He greatly enjoyed his fellowship with the
warm-hearted blacksmith. But in spite of all his excellent qualities, it is to be feared that the other Joseph
—his brother—was a man of the world, one whose portion was in this life only. He sometimes spoke dis-
respectfully of the Bible, and abused religious people.
He had no sympathy with the new line his brother had
taken. In consequence Howell could hardly feel free to
open his heart in his letters to London as he does in the
diary. In the latter he writes as if on wings in the

spacious heavens; but in the former his feet are generally firmly on earth. Yet, in spite of his respect for his brother, his greatest benefactor, he would not be unfaithful to his convictions in order to win anybody's approbation. He wrote to his brother early in June, and, among other things, he said:

I am very much oblig'd to you for your sudden answer, but your not hearing from Mr. Harte since does not give me so much uneasiness as formerly less matters did. . . . I don't in ye least fear or Doubt of a Livelyhood and such a one as a better Judge than Man will see best, . . . I hope I am design'd for some publick good, nor shall I think any labour or Pain too much for my qualifying me for such a Work, but if I find no other approbation than Human I shall hardly think all Qualifications sufficient. I pity poor Mankind and wish I could do good to all, but now my wish is all and I hope my own Heart is at last made Steady and Unshaken by ye frowns or Smiles of Fortune. I hope ye applause or Censure of ye world shall never touch me so near as it has. . . .

Don't think me to be so Melancholy as you Imagine; I enjoy a Treasure of Joy which Indeed I can't know how to communicate, (Grief is allmost a stranger). I would not exchange Conditions with a great many that seem to be happier than I am. . . . It is not lowness of Spirit but an Alteration in Notions and Principles and Resolutions that makes me so applaud solitude and Despise Riches to Excess. No, I have got a great Degree of what I would wish all had—Content, inward undisturbed Happiness grounded, I hope, on true Humility. . . .

Allow me so much seriousness as sincerely to deal honestly and justly with my soul, and make my eternal Happiness sure; and then I'll with as much cheerfullness as you please be your Companion, and am happy of Course here. But 'tis to be lamented that this Happiness pure and Conscious is grown such an obsolete talk, that he is a Subject of Ridicule that offers to start it in Discourse or

B

Letter; speak no where of it but in the Pulpit. But where there are those of my way of thinking, I long to be acquainted with them. If I found such a Person I'd sooner part with Life than such a Precious gem.

You see I am unshaken in my Resolutions and therefore don't dissuade me, but direct me in this road, . . .[1]

Joseph visited Wales in the autumn, and before he came down Howell wrote to him as follows:

When you come here you shall hear various opinions of me; some call me melancholy, some mad, and some are so favourable to me as to give me ye greatest Title, of being religious, but (Thank God) they are all alike to me. Applause is not my study. Nothing affects me more that ye Precious Time I abus'd, which I am endeavouring to redeem as fast as I can.

"At present, I am where I was the first year," said Harris once, "without any creature between me and God." It cost him dearly to reach this height inasmuch as "one creature" had already won a special place in his heart. The most prominent and the most important person, perhaps, in the parish of Llangasty at that time was Mrs. Parry, of Tal-y-llyn Mansion.[2] She was the lady of the manor, and the patroness of the ecclesiastical living. She was a young widow, of good character, and in very comfortable circumstances.[3] But the poor schoolmaster's heart ventured to cross the social gulf, and there

---

[1] These quotations are exactly as found in the English diaries of Howell Harris. This old English style of course does not appear where translation has been made from Harris's diaries written in Latin and Welsh.—Pub.

[2] Called Tal-y-llyn House, or the Manor House, by Theophilus Jones, *Hist. of Breckonshire* (Glanusk Ed.), iii. 217.

[3] She is addressed "Mrs. M. Parry" in his letter to her, dated 26 Aug. 1737. According to the Llangasty parish registers, "James Parry, Gent was buried the 30th day of December 1732." His wife was Mary, daughter and co-heiress of Howel Jones of Brecon (see Theophilus Jones, *op. cit.*, iv. 3).

commenced a repetition of the story of Syfaddan of old, in exactly the same place. We cannot say when Mrs. Parry came to know of the affectionate homage paid to her. I believe that she is darkly referred to in the desire for a "friend" in some of Harris's letters in the beginning of summer, 1735. He writes:

> I Think a Friend is, if such a thing to be found, ye greatest Happiness we can enjoy here. . . . I am in Raptures when I read in Milton ye Friendship between our first Parents before self Designs came to ye World. I almost utterly Despair of having this gem in this World. . . . But there is an unsurmountable obstacle in my Way, viz. Meaness of estate. . . . But, I think that Happiness is come so far to my sight that I can say I am in hopes of attaining it, . . . and perhaps when I am just entering to my Happiness I am knock'd off so that Perhaps I am to be allways swimming but never reaching ye shore. . . . I have done all I can to find such a Thing, but never could amongst my equals. If by favour and admittance I thought I saw those Qualities of such a Friend I long'd for in superiors, there Fortune would stare me in ye Face, and when I had a mind to utter something ye fear of being term'd a fool designing or an Impudent made me stifle my notions for fear of Disobliging.

He gave up Mrs. Parry, as he did everything else; but he once confesses that his affection for her mingled in his thoughts, at times, with more spiritual matters. When his brother came home, he and Howell, I believe, visited Tal-y-llyn, and in future "———" is often mentioned in his papers. She had considerable influence on Harris, for the most part wholesome, until her death in 1738; and he grieved bitterly after her. It is strange that not one of his biographers refers to the first patroness—if not, indeed, the fiancée—of their hero—*The Lady of the Lake*.

IN OXFORD

(November 1735)

SINCE it is wellnigh impossible to decipher[1] the Latin diaries, this chapter again will contain an imperfect record. It seems that Harris had no strong inclination to enter the university after his conversion. In a letter to his brother, written in May, he says: "I Thirst for Improvement but I have had such a Notion of an Oxford Life that I am in a strait what to do, but as I know you'll conscientiously tender my future Happiness . . . I'll be entirely directed by your advice." In the autumn when his brother returned to London, Howell accompanied him to Oxford. For all we know to the contrary, it was intended that he should remain there for a term; we have no explanation of his leaving the place before the week was out apart from the following quotations: "In November I was taken to Oxford, but the Lord brought me again from there. I entered my name at St. Margaret Hall. I took the oath of allegiance to his Majesty the King the day I matriculated. When I began to wear better clothes, my pride revived, and I lost some of my watchfulness. I soon tired of the place, and I longed for my freedom, which I soon obtained. I came home, and my brother offered to have me to live with him; but God had such a hold on me that I could not go. Soon afterwards I left my school, and I devoted myself to exhorting everyone I met to flee from the wrath to come."

As far as he himself was concerned, Harris, I believe, bade farewell for ever to Oxford at that time. But it

[1] See footnote, page 28.

seems that his brother did not agree that his connection with the university should end so suddenly, not necessarily for educational reasons, but because of the advantage which an Oxford degree would give him in entering the ministry. There are a few references to this matter in the family correspondence which has survived, and we place them here before the reader.

Joseph to Howell, 31 May 1735:

I received yours which I am sorry to find So full of melancholy reflections. You Should not quarrel with the world before you know it, and instead of talking of retirement at Your age, You should rather resolve to undertake with chearfullness whatever Providence may throw in Your way. You do not want for capacity, and a willing mind and an upright heart are the best qualifications for any undertaking. If you was in orders, I might easier do something for you that way than any other. There are Livings to be disposed of often, but preferment of other kind are very Scarce. I do not think Logick to be of much, if it is of any use, but a degree from the University may be of use to a Clergyman, and upon that account I Should have been glad if You could get one without Spending much time for it.

Howell to Joseph, 30 December 1735:

I don't know whether it be advisable to come [to Talgarth to keep a school] against y^c Parson's approbation and to begin before I go once to Oxon, . . . I should be glad to know if possible when I shall be called to Oxford. Some Oxonians here advise me to keep three Terms at once and go up in March that then I may be dispensed with for a whole twelve month and that ye three Terms may be kept with ten or twelve weeks.

Joseph to his mother, 17 January 1736:

I hope Now he [Howell] is in a fair way of doing well, and I fancy he is pleased with his Oxford Journey, where he is to go again Some time in the Spring.

Howell to Joseph, 21 January 1736:

Mrs. A[nne Jones, of Tredwstan] offered me yᵉ Reading of some Books, but I am tyed up to Latin and Greek you know. I have been reading Pearson on yᵉ Creed for some time which I shall have done with next week. Then I intend to fall to my Classicks. . . . I shan't think my time lost as long as I have Books but this unavoidable evil of Classical Study must take my Time for yᵉ Future. Mr. Hart and your self know best when I am to go to Oxford.

Joseph to Howell, 24 January 1736:

You'll find in this Box an old Suit of mine which my brother has altered for you with two pair of Breeches belonging to it, also my old leather breeches. These may do you a good deal of Service for common wear either in the Countrey or at Oxford. Your old clothes are so bad you had better give them away, if they are worth any body's having.

Joseph to Howell, 20 March 1736:

I Suppose You'll go to Oxford against next term, when it begins I do not justly know, but Mr. Harte will inform me.

Joseph to Howell, 24 April 1736:

The next term at Oxford begins the 5th of May, but I am intirely of your Sentiment that you had best Stay till Talgarth School is vacant, and try if you can get into Orders before you go there; all that may be done before the Succeeding term.

Harris offered himself for orders in July 1736, but he was churlishly refused because of his activity in going about the country to exhort. He preferred to renounce everything rather than to cease from warning his fellow-men of their danger; and he thought little or nothing afterwards about going to the university. It is true that, at times, in view of the positive opposition of Church- men, and of some Nonconformists, to a lay ministry, a wave of depression would overwhelm him and he would speak of giving up his work, or of entering upon a fur- ther course of education in order to fit himself for orders in the Established Church. But he would not remain long in his cave. In spite of his saying, as Jeremiah of old, that he would speak no more in the name of the Lord, the Word was as fire in his bones, and the sight of the multitude indulging themselves in frivolity and dis- sipation, or a request for help from some Cornelius would cause the flame to blaze as brightly as ever.

It is stated in *A Brief Account of the Life of Howell Harris,*[1] that Harris stayed a whole term at Oxford. This, of course, is incorrect. Mr. Beriah Gwynfe Evans, in his book, *The Reformers of Wales,*[2] was the first to draw attention to this inaccuracy. But Mr. Evans is mistaken when he makes Harris himself responsible for this inaccurate statement. The original manuscript is lost. The book was printed in 1791, and it is unfair to hold an author responsible for any inaccuracies which appear in a work published nearly twenty years after his death. It is difficult enough to get a faultless work through the press even when the author is alive and can correct the proof-sheets. John Wesley complained bit- terly of printers' errors. They distorted the meaning completely in many instances in his writings. He thought of publishing a correct edition of his works before he died, but he failed miserably in his endeavours.[3] If it

[1] Published in 1791, and printed by the Trevecka Press— G. M. R.

[2] *Diwygwyr Cymru,* 1900; a contentious book which provoked much controversy amongst Welsh historians when it first ap- peared.—G. M. R.

[3] See John Wesley, *Works,* preface to the third edition.

is not right to hold Mr. Wesley responsible for the inaccuracies in his works, much less should we hold Howell Harris responsible for any inaccuracies in the autobiography. It is known that editors in the old days, as well as printers, took much liberty with the writings of deceased authors,[1] and there is reason to believe that this happened with Harris's papers. In the autobiography, a number of letters were included, the originals of which still exist. On these we can still see the marks of the pen of the editor—whoever he was—deleting paragraphs and inserting words here and there so that the meaning is slightly changed in some sentences. It is possible that what was done with the letters was also done with the other part of the book. But the most likely explanation is that the editor has misread one word in the author's manuscript, which, as Mr. Evans notes, is full of abbreviations and difficult to decipher. It is much easier to believe this than to suppose that a man like Harris was mistaken, or that he deliberately misleads his readers on a point of fact while leaving behind him so many proofs that would bring the inaccuracy to light. What end would be gained by leading anyone to believe that he had stayed six weeks in Oxford, while complaining at the same time of the ungodliness of the place? It is well known that from his conversion to his death he attached greater importance to godliness than to learning; and his temptation surely would be to shorten, rather than to lengthen, his stay in such a place.[2]

[1] See Dr. Calamy, *Life and Times,* 2nd Ed., Vol. I, pp. 377-8, 447-51.
[2] Mr. Evans, the author of *The Reformers of Wales,* was not sympathetic to the convictions held by Howell Harris, and because of the widespread circulation of the book Bennett considered it necessary to repudiate some of his allegations in detail. We have included his treatment of this matter in an Appendix (see p. 184).—Pub.

HIS FIRST CAMPAIGN

(December 1735—February 1736)

When Harris was in the throes of his great crisis, fighting against the temptation to Atheism, the thought came to him sometimes that God must be a splendid Master, and that it would be wonderful to serve Him—if he could but believe in Him. In spite of the fact that the strong man armed had been cast out in May, he was not divested of all his armour at once. But in December, in reading Pearson on the Creed, the remaining roots of unbelief were completely removed from Harris's heart, and he yielded himself and his members anew to the Almighty. By now he had relinquished his school at Llangasty. He also gave up fasting as unprofitable; he stopped praying from a book, and soon gave up reading, since he had no longer any leisure. "Now [December] a strong necessity was laid upon me, that I could not rest, but must go to the utmost of my ability to exhort. I could not meet or travel with anybody, rich or poor, young or old, without speaking to them of religion and concerning their souls. Persuaded by my neighbours, I went during the festive season from house to house in our parish, and the parishes of Llan-gors and Llangasty, until persecution became too hot. I was absolutely dark and ignorant with regard to the reasons of religion; I was drawn onwards by the love I had experienced, as a blind man is led, and therefore I could not take notice of anything in my way. My food and drink was praising my God. A fire was kindled in my soul and I was clothed with power and made altogether dead to all earthly things. I could have spoken to the King were he within reach—such power and authority did I feel in my soul over every spirit. . . . I lifted up my voice with authority, and fear and terror would be seen on all faces. I went to the Talgarth fairs denouncing the swearers and cursers without fear or favour. At first I knew nothing at all, but God opened my mouth (full of ignorance), filling it with terrors and threatenings. I was given a commission to break and rend sinners in the most dreadful manner. I thundered greatly, denouncing the gentry, the carnal clergy, and everybody. My subjects, mostly, were death and judgment, without any mention of Christ. I had no order, and hardly any time to read, except a few pages now and then, because of constant busyness and haste. But when I came to the people matter enough was given to me, and I received fluency of speech and great earnestness, although I was inclined by nature to levity and frivolity."

His usual method was to commence by reading the Lord's Prayer, or the Creed, or a chapter from *The Whole Duty of Man*, or some other book; and then he would speak by way of exposition on what had been read, allowing himself to be led with complete passivity under the extraordinary inspiration which possessed him at that time. He began to speak hundreds of times without having any idea as to what he was going to say. He would go on thus, pouring out old things and new for two, three, or even four hours. Indeed, we have instances of his services continuing without a break for six hours. Possibly the meetings were briefer in this, his first campaign, but, according to his own opinion, his ministry was never more powerful than it was then. His highest praise for his most outstanding services at the peak of his influence was to say that "the power of the first year has returned." Many innocent people thought that all they heard came from a book, and he made no attempt to correct this impression. He was very much afraid of undertaking a work which he was not authorised to do, and so did all he could to avoid the semblance of "preaching." Thus, for the first two years, his practice was to go from place to place "reading." He did not make much use of the Bible in those days. In spite of his reverence for it, for a long time Satan worked in him a curious disinclination to use the Word of God. Nevertheless, he often refers to certain scriptures, such as that word in Jeremiah, "But I have made Esau bare, I have uncovered his secret places, and he shall not be able to hide himself."[1] It would be difficult to find a better description of his own ministry in the early days, and indeed, to some extent, throughout his life, than what is expressed in that verse.

The first gift he received was one of "similitudes and apt comparisons." They were all very simple and easily understood by the dullest of his hearers. Someone out on the open mountain having lost his way, and darkness overtaking him. A house on fire with the door locked, and the family refusing to open the door, etc. Such things spiritualised, flowing out scorching hot from the speaker's heart, would leave a wonderful effect on the minds of many of his hearers. He was very acceptable for some weeks. But as the novelty wore away, and when he himself began to particularise, pouncing upon the besetting sins of the age and the particular locality, some were disgusted and others were terrified. Vicar Davies opposed him from the beginning, and now he took advantage of his opportunity and sent him a nasty, imperious letter commanding him to give up the work immediately and warning him that he would lose the favour of his brother and others, together with every hope of obtaining Holy Orders. At the same time a more

[1] Jer. 49:10.

friendly Justice of the Peace advised him to beware of Puritanical zeal, and the people were threatened that they would be fined £20 for admitting him to their houses. It was in the face of such things that Harris's first public attack on the ramparts of the enemy came to an end in February 1736, after lasting barely three months.

He might have addressed his opposers in the words spoken to Eliab of old, "What have I now done? Is there not a cause?" During these months he wrote to his brother reproaching him with regard to his religious ideas. He writes:

> I hope as to Religion you are not what you seem to be, some expressions of yours return so upon me that when I am merriest they make me serious. . . . I sincerely wish you would read more Divinity. . . . Yᵉ Scandalous character of yᵉ Clergy can't invalidate their Doctrine, Tho' some of them are contemptible Creatures, Religion must not suffer for that. Christ's commands are as authentick now as when He was on Earth, . . . I think there is a Spark within my Breast which fairly begins to kindle, which if I shall be able to keep alive, must in its own Nature shew it self in Time and I hope to ye publick good. . . . My being so long in yᵉ Country has given me an opportunity to make my observations on man from yᵉ highest to yᵉ Lowest, and I have hardly met a man that rightly understands what a soul is, much less its faculties: yᵉ Rich are employ'd about their diversion etc., yᵉ Drunkard, Dancer or yᵉ Huntsman is yᵉ only Man of Repute.

It seems that much success attended his labours before the vicar's opposition came into the open. In writing to Mrs. Parry he says:

> What gave me yᵉ greatest Satisfaction was your non-opposition of that Heavenly work I took in Hand which [showed] itself to all but such as were blind, were it only

ye success of it, and the interruption I met in it by those in Authority, when I had Surmounted all the Reproach of false [names] they Honoured me with, gave me great inward uneasiness, and I desisted not out of fear of them, for that I had learnt long ago to surmount, but least I should be said to resist Authority, or be supposed to Commit a crime.

In a letter written to his brother, dated 29 March 1736, he says:

God has done great Things for you and, if I could stoop to be a Schoolboy Scholar again for a twelve-month, I see something in myself much above my Birth. God imparts greatness often where 'tis least expected and there 'tis the more conspicuous and greater glory redounds to Him. . . . I have my share of sweets and bitters every day, but my Happiness is within myself. Y^e Private Joys of a Religious Life are rather Conceivable than to be describ'd. That, with Content and ye Satisfaction I enjoy in ye Society and favour of —— [Mrs. Parry?] makes me easy amidst many Waves That beat upon me. Y^e Reformation of so many People has drawn upon me ye Envy of some mean, narrow thinking Parsons (tho' none that know me), who endeavour to disturb my Peace as much as they can, and seem already to dread ye Piety and True Christian Zeal of one who being not guilty of their Practices may not be afraid to expose 'em in Time. If thereby any good can be done.

N.B.—When I was stricken, about February, 1736, I thought I was dying, and I could not but be joyful, longing for my dissolution.

It is not known whether this was a bout of sickness or something resulting from persecution, but its effects lasted for some weeks. On 20 March 1736 he wrote to Mrs. Parry:

When first I had incurred your Indignation at the discovery of which I was not able to hide any Longer, I was fully resolved to give you no further Room to be offended on that account, but such was ye yearning that I felt I could not help sometimes to enjoy that happiness of seeing you, which now I see ye folly of. My Desires were so Honourable and love of such an uncommon nature that I own I make no Apologie for it, but to the Contrary. . . . I write after having had some infallible signs of an approaching Death and have order'd they should not be deliver'd till after my Death and that by a Hand you can trust, tho' much I wish'd to see you, but was afraid to raise confusion in you, and that I should part with this world in your favour which next with God's I have always been most desirous to retain.

Within a week he was restored to such an extent as to be able to visit Tal-y-llyn, spending a day or two there most comfortably.

As it has been already suggested, he half-expected an appointment to a school in Talgarth at this time. During his stay in the district the previous autumn, Joseph Harris had visited a gentleman named Counsellor Williams, in whose hands lay the chief control of the school. It seems that there was a disagreement with regard to education in Talgarth at the time, and that one party was withholding its subscriptions for some reason. As a result the schoolmaster gave notice of his resignation, as he could not live on the reduced salary. In order to keep the school going Counsellor Williams suggested to his visitor that the place would well suit his brother— that he would probably give greater general satisfaction and gain monetary support from the disaffected party. But the old schoolmaster was unwilling to leave when it came to the point. Harris wrote to his brother:

I told you in my Last ye particulars about my School and I saw ye Councellor Since that. He seems resolv'd to turn ye Schoolmaster away after a quarter's notice, but I don't know whether it be advisable to come against ye Parson's approbation, . . . I should be glad to know if possible, . . . that I may give an answer to ye Councellor, least he should turn that man away in ye meantime and give ye School to another Master. . . . I am very much censur'd now for attempting (as they call it) to take away ye poor Schoolmaster's Bread, and really it carries some guilt with it, for twas not fair. . . . I must see ye Councellor soon. He, I believe, would do anything in his Power to my advantage as ye Vicar would to ye Contrary, but still there is a Being that over rules all and in Him I repose my present and future Tranquility.

CONSORTING WITH THE NONCONFORMISTS
(March-May 1736)

In the previous chapter we left Harris in tribulation, and in a sorry plight. His health, it seems, was impaired; his money was all spent; he depended on his brother's generosity for decent clothing; and he looked in vain for a place as a schoolmaster, with a salary of four pounds a year. He had been partly hindered from proceeding with the work which he loved more than life itself; there was no man in the district of Talgarth who could be so easily dispensed with. But all this was the beginning of afflictions, and worse things were to follow. After being wounded in the house of his friends, he was now encouraged to go on by people whom he had once despised.

Harris was a zealous churchman. There was a time when he reckoned as fools—or worse—all who did not attend the Church. In her communion he had first met with God; and the substance of his exhortations, at first, had been to persuade people to attend her services. He highly revered her ministers, and his chief desires during these first months were for their awakening. But now they, above all others, were joined together in one force against him, cautioning their people to avoid him as if he were a mad dog, and driving him out of their parishes. "The ministers preached against me as a false prophet, the people despised me, pointing at me as I passed by, and young wastrels threatened to murder me, speaking all kinds of falsehoods against me. I was persecuted at home, too, and continually expected to be

turned out of doors. I was threatened with imprison-
ment many times. In order to keep me humble the Lord
made me a laughing-stock and a subject of lampoons to
all." It was many years later that he wrote thus, and
perhaps the description is coloured somewhat by the
fiercer opposition that he met with in later years.

A congregation of Independents used to meet at
Tredwstan, near his home. After he began his public
work he became acquainted with some of their leading
people, and he received more encouragement from them
than from the leaders of his own people. His strong
bigotry had already receded before the stronger love that
ruled in his heart. He desired and prayed to be the
means of unifying all the Lord's people, though he saw
no sign of this ever happening. "Since I received the
Spirit of God, whenever I felt a prejudice for or against
any sect I always knew it had come from the devil and
my own heart, and I could not rest in it any more than
I could in hell. Such a thought never came from Jesus."
But he knew, too, that the common people were filled
with prejudice and zeal for the Church, and lest he
should stir up this spirit and thus hinder his own influence, he kept away from the Nonconformist meeting
places on Sundays, attending only the Church services.
But almost from the beginning of his ministry he consorted with them on week-days, and we find him lodging
with one of them before the end of his first campaign.

Some years before this, William Herbert, one of the
members of Tredwstan, had changed his mind with regard to the method of baptism, and who should be the
proper subjects of the ordinance, and had joined the Baptists. It seems that William Herbert was more cultured
in mind and more devotional in spirit than ordinary
professors of religion, and was now about to undertake
the public work at Trosgoed. In March 1736 Harris

met him somewhere, and for some time after that he often refers to him. As far as we can judge, the Baptists were livelier and more industrious during these years than any other sect—excepting perhaps the Papists. Their vigour and fervour impressed Harris very much, and we find him more than once entertaining the thought of throwing in his lot with them. But they placed more emphasis upon their own ideas concerning baptism than on other matters of far greater importance, in his view; and as a result many of them were possessed by a prosely-tising spirit. In the diaries, complaints are constantly made against them, suggesting that they should rather direct their efforts towards the ungodly world, leaving in peace people already professing the Christian faith in other denominations. It seems that William Herbert and Philip Morgan (the minister of Trosgoed) tried to persuade him to join with them when they first met. In spite of all this, it is quite evident that Harris considered it a great blessing to have become acquainted with William Herbert at this time.

Although Harris would not allow any personal advantage or disadvantage, which might have resulted from his work of exhorting, to affect his resolution, yet he sometimes hesitated about the course which he should take. His regard for all authority, civil and ecclesiastical, together with a fear of being guilty of resisting it, often kept him on tenterhooks. Indeed, this was the greatest perplexity of his life. Outward sufferings were as noth-ing compared with the overwhelming anxiety which now oppressed him from this direction. If the vicar did not succeed in silencing him, he succeeded in causing him untold misery. He reasoned and consulted with people, and prayed incessantly about the matter. He even kept a keen watch over his dreams in order to find some hint from above on how to steer his course. At last, on the

morning of the last day but one of March, we find him
venturing to ask his Heavenly Father for a sign, that he
might be certain of his way. "Inasmuch as spiritual
reason causes me to read[1] [*i.e.* in public], and human
reason prohibits me," he writes, "I humbly prayed if my
confidence was not presumptuous, for an infallible sign
in order to know if God was commanding me to read, at
least until Easter, and promising His blessing upon it.
. . . As Thy Spirit formerly utterly convinced me of
Thy pardon and favour, He can also, in this, give me
complete assurance beyond all doubting. And as I constantly find that tears, tenderness, and a longing love
within me are the effects of Thy Divine Spirit, and that
I cannot at any time thus soften my own heart, and that
the morning is the most sluggish period of the day with
me; thus, if it be Thy will that I should read other than
on Sundays, may it please Thee to show this to me in an
unmistakable way by softening me this moment with Thy
Spirit. If this be not granted unto me, I will desist,
knowing that Thou art pleased with what I have already
done, and that Thou art commanding me to follow the
ordinary procedure to qualify myself for orders. I know
that Thou hast often heard me, and answered me, by
performing such wonders—melting so many hard hearts,
which no one could formerly convince. I know Thy
power; if I could but know Thy will, then I should be
at peace. . . . Then, after I had waited long, when I
was about to stand on my feet—Oh! glad tidings—the
Spirit descended with tears and unusual tenderness, an
infallible assurance that I was to continue reading at
least until Easter. Then I vowed that I would read in
spite of swords, fire, or fierce wrath, without fear of being
rent in pieces, leaning completely on God for every quali-

[1] This refers to his practice of reading from some religious
book, while exhorting (see page 43).—Pub.

fication, yet without neglecting to do all I could to that end during the periods when I could not read. I am now assured of Thy command, and of Thy blessing, Thy protection and Thy favour; and without any fear for the future I give myself, body, soul, and reputation, unto Thee. I cast myself upon Thee; guide me aright. Behold me an instrument in Thy hand. Oh! ye angels, sing His praises now louder than ever before, because He hath visited me in the day of my trouble." This happened on the anniversary of the morning when he was first convicted in Talgarth church, when his steps were halted in the broad way.

The result of the opposition of the vicar and others was to extend the new movement's boundaries. After they had prohibited the public readings, the reader doubled his diligence, going about the country to private readings. He went to the surrounding districts— Llanfihangel, Trefidde, Tyle-crwn, Talach-ddu, Cathedin, and the mountainous district towards Grwyne Fawr and Grwyne Fechan. He now went about mostly by night, in order not to arouse the anger of the enemy against his innocent hearers. With a continual supply of subject matter, and power from above, the Word was constantly on his lips, and he was not concerned about anything else. He was rewarded by having unusually close and constant communion with God. As afflictions multiplied his comforts multiplied more abundantly. He speaks again and again of a spiritual feast which he enjoyed about this time on Grwyne Fechan mountain while returning home from Cwm Iau, when he seemed to see God so smiling upon him that his heart was near to bursting under the powerful influences of Divine Love. The place became a holy mountain to him ever afterwards.

The opposition waxed stronger continually. "The

Nonconformists began to take notice of me, encouraging me; I was now being called one of them, because I consorted with them. Afterwards there was a great forsaking; very few remained with me, and almost everybody turned against me in persecution. . . . Where is the Lord? Oh! stand for Thy cause. Why should the ungodly triumph against Thy servant, who has nothing in view but the prosperity of godliness and religion! If God blesses the Word, why should they begrudge me a blessing because I am poor, preventing me from drawing souls unto Him, especially as one of the ways I use to draw, is the same as their own? The next age will have a strange conception of ours, when they hear of the opposition that godliness suffers from its own professors. I told W. A. that I was fairly hopeful that I would soon die, or else perform great things. From the bottom of my heart, I would die rather than give up reading, and instructing the ignorant." Just before Easter, Mary Perrot, one of his followers, was affected with a kind of frenzy. The same thing happened to others, too, after this, when the influences were very powerful. But probably she was the first, and in spite of many prayers offered on her behalf we do not know that she was ever restored. This gave occasion to the enemies to rage, and to blaspheme against the work of the revival more than ever.

Harris, however, was not disturbed or discouraged, but sometimes he wrote bitter things against his enemies. "I think it a sin to allow personal gain to vie with public good. If the latter is aimed at sincerely, it must be done without a thought for the former. I fear that we have many who wear the cloth more with a view to enriching themselves, and enjoying an easy life, than to the promotion of the common good. They succeed in getting rich but what good they do I know not—let the unbiased judge. Because I led some hundreds of ignorant people to a knowledge of their duties, and what it means to be Christians—to live in peace and concord and to exercise morality, I am threatened and called a madman, etc., by those who claim the office of enlightening the people who are in darkness. They are more contemptible than ordinary business men, who, when they see another doing better business, try to imitate his methods. What have I taken from them, or what have I gained? Their churches are fuller, and they are revered more than before. I love the religion, but I must despise these niggardly professors. Do I fear their rage? What can they set against me, except that I have endeavoured to do good, and that God has followed my efforts with His blessing, which they do not seek and cannot receive. They are affronted because people say that they receive more benefit by listening to me than to them. There must be some worthy men in the world of the same mind as myself. Until I meet with such to encourage me, I will go on with such support as I have. Were I to be ordained, I could not claim to be the means of salvation to more than one parish! but now, through God's help, I could save many, were I given authority."

The following quotations from his correspondence with his brother shed light on his circumstances about May 1736:

Fortune is resolved to qualify me by her sudden Turns for greater Disappointment; ye Schoolmaster has re-apply'd for ye School again and since he was for it I think it no Point of honesty to turn him off, if I could. . . . Tho' I know not in the least how Providence will dispose of me, yet I am as easy as if I had ye School and am well assur'd tis better, as tho' at present I can't prove it, yet Time will shew it. . . . Some say ye Bishop comes to his Diocese about Midsummer, but I am told he ordains none till upwards of

6 months above 22, which will be an Objection to me, if
I could in other Respects come off, which I have not assurance enough to trust. . . . I have not one Friend to write
with me or recommend me, none of my Friends being
acquainted with his Lordship.   W. Badham and Wm.
Games (being repuls'd here) have been admitted at London.   Whether I am sufficient Master of ye Languages or
not, I can't tell, I can Construe ye Greek Testament pretty
well, but ye Latin is copious and a Retentive Faculty I
was never Master of. . . . With regard to my character,
those clergymen who know me have nothing to set against
me; some of ye Fraternity are apprehensive by my singular
Piety.   So I must expect all Drunkards, Topers and negli-
gent Part of ye Clergy (and you may imagine to what a
number they will amount to) will set their staves across y^e
Door, least Vertue should come in and set their darling
Vice out in their proper Colours; I never gave offence to
any of 'em in publick or in Private.   Notwithstanding if
some poor ignorant sick Person sends for me and I go and
read a little there about Universal Charity, Sobriety, etc.,
their Envy must shew it self at hearing ye poor People
speaking well of me, etc., for my Charity, Piety, etc.   They
call me a Dissenter because I won't condemn 'em all to
hell, etc., or because I converse some times with some of
them. . . . I know not what steps to take; if you would
advise me you do well.

Perhaps the reader is surprised that Harris, at this
time, had not become a Nonconformist.   Truly, he was
in sore straits on all sides.   Were he to stay in the Established Church his work would most likely be hindered
for a long time, and he would be restricted in the end to
the parochial sphere.   If he joined the Nonconformists,
that again would restrict him, because the majority of
the people would have nothing to do with Nonconformity
at that time.   The most likely, if not indeed the only
way, of influencing the multitudes was to keep some
kind of connection with the Church.   Moreover, he had

begun his mission within her fold. He gathered from this that the Lord meant to revive her—possibly through his instrumentality; and he felt very unwilling to desert her. "To convince the world of the power of my principles, and of my attachment to the Established Church, I did not take a licence, neither did I use licensed buildings, which is easily done. This is not a part of our beliefs." It is possible that the influence of his brother, Mrs. Parry and others also tended to keep him in the Church.

At last the time drew near for him to become acquainted with Churchmen who "were worthy men, of the same mind as himself." He first heard of Griffith Jones, Llanddowror, in May, from some Independents of Tredwstan, possibly. He wrote to his brother:

> I have been Inform'd there is a Clergymen in Caermarthenshire, one Mr. Griffith Jones, a great man; he marry'd Sir John Phillips' sister, who is of this extraordinary turn, he devotes himself entirely to ye Duties of his Function. He is such another in some respect as ye good man of Ross. If I could be introduc'd to him he could befriend me; he would draw my Character in its due Light to ye Bishop and easily answer ye objection of Non age and Imperfection in ye learned Languages, etc. If I can come to be known to him it must be thro' ye Dissenters, for ye Clergy hate him for his singular Piety and Charity to ye Dissenters, etc. I have spoken to some but have not determin'd about going to see him. I intend to wait upon Mr. Jones, Vicar of Cwmyoe [Cwm Iau], who is ye only one of ye same way of thinking, and I am told he corresponds with Mr. Griffith Jones.

WITH THE WORTHY CHURCHMEN
(May-June 1736)

OF the few faithful ones left in the Established Church in that degenerate age, the best known are the two men referred to at the end of the previous chapter. Mr. Jones of Llanddowror is to this day a family name in Wales,[1] so that there is no need to go into the details of his history here. Very little is known of the vicar of Cwm Iau;[2] but we can gather something of his life and character from a letter he wrote to George Whitefield in April 1739.

> I rarely meet with a Brother of ye same Communion who so exactly corresponds with me in Principles,—one who so harmoniously concurrs with my notions in Religion. . . . But as for our Doctrine of Regeneration I always observe that it sounds as a Paradox to all those that are not subjects of it in ye genuine sense of ye words and are not born from Above. . . . But man—poor, proud and bankrupt, ten thousand talents in debt and nothing to pay—naturally would fain be a participant in Christ, and can hardly be brought so low as to confess himself an unprofitable servant. Moreover, he will not drink of the

[1] Two works in English have been published lately on Griffith Jones, viz. (a) F. A. Cavenagh, *The Life and Work of Griffith Jones* (1930); (b) Thomas Kelly, *Griffith Jones, Llanddowror; Pioneer in Adult Education* (1950). Both are published by the University of Wales Press, Cardiff.—G. M. R.

[2] A memorial tablet in Cwm Iau Church records that he was the curate of that parish for fifty years, from 1719 until his death. He was also the vicar of Eardesland in the county of Hereford. He died in March 1772, aged 83. Cwm Iau is an isolated parish in the Black Mountains, on the confines of Monmouthshire, Breconshire, and Herefordshire. It is not far from Llanthony Abbey about 12 miles from Talgarth, as the crow flies.—G. M. R.

water of life freely; although he has no money, yet, to be sure, he will offer any price, he will plead a little merit. . . . This is yᵉ Good old Puritan Doctrine that to my great concern I thought had quite forsaken yᵉ Land till about 14 months ago I met with some of your Sermons . . . but my more perfect attachment to you, dear Sir, commenced upon my reading a little while since your Journal to Georgia where I observed that your affections clave to yᵉ Scotch Societys at Gibraltar, tho' of different sentiments in Religion with these of yᵉ Established Church, when with some warmth and vehemency you seem to brake out into these expressions that it was a pity that yᵉ seamless Coat of Christ should be rent, with which words I felt such a Qualm on my Spirits with such promptness to conclude "here is a Rara Avis," a Brother indeed that can be in Love with yᵉ Divine Stamp in whom so ever he beholds it. . . . I thought I could with yᵉ same sincerity say to you as Ruth did to Naomi, "Whither so ever thou goest I will go," etc., for I thought my natural affection to my Relations were so swallowed up in Spiritual Affections to you, but those to my poor flock would not suffer me to quit my station.

The first Subject I ever preached upon was "Oh! taste and see that yᵉ Lord is good," etc., when I tho't I had such experiences of good to my soul that if I could but be instrumental to prevail upon yᵉ most abandoned wretch to taste it would be no longer in his Choice whether he would be religious or no. But Oh! good God, what Changes have I met with since, what tossings up and down! I was cast into yᵉ lowest pit, into yᵉ deep; all his waves and billows went over my Soul, without hope in yᵉ world, forsaken of God. To read yᵉ promises was only to provoke my envy to those to whom they belonged, and increasing my grief and misery. . . . I thought of God and I was disturbed; my judgment went past him; he had forgotten how to have mercy upon me, and my soul refused to be comforted. In my opinion, his promise towards me had ceased for ever. Heman's psalm[1] alone was appro-

---

[1] Psalm 88.—Pub.

priate to my state, and an occasional verse from Job and Lamentations. At last I gave up ye ministry, as if it did not belong to me to speak of his testimonies, or to take his law upon my defiled lips. Thus his greatness turned me in the prison house.

But at last he that will not always Chide nor keep his anger for ever put off my Sackcloth, turned my mourning into Dancing, and in a still small voice about two years afterwards whispered to my Soul, "Thy sins are forgiven." He seemed to embrace my soul with his left Hand under my head, and his right hand a-caressing me—his manhood and his Godhead engaged for my comfort and happiness. Then I could say that "my Beloved was mine and I was his." How vile I was in my own sight! How elevated my soul! And how splendid was free grace!

Such was Thomas Jones of Cwm Iau. He was a burning and a shining light in a very dark age; but the range of his shining was more restricted than that of Griffith Jones. We know very little of that man's inner history. But if we are not mistaken he, too, had experienced conversion in the distant past; one of his acquaintances told Howell Harris that he was quite dead, as regards his body, for about two hours at that time. It is likely that the personal experiences of the two men had a bearing upon the character of their ministry. They both preached justification by faith, giving prominence to Divine Grace, which was a very uncommon thing in those days. Yet they were far from being indifferent to conduct. There was a strong element of severity and seriousness in both of them, more so than in any of the ministers that Harris had listened to. "Was it not Free Grace which brought me into touch with the saints—to know Mr. Griffith Jones, that I might be searched to the depths; and Mr. Jones, Cwm Iau, to know a detailed examination?" But it was not through them that he was led to embrace the Doctrine of Grace, as we shall see later on.

At the end of May 1736, at the suggestion of Mr. Williams, the minister of Tredwstan,[1] and Mr. Williams of Rhos, one of his members, Harris set off for Llanddowror. There is no indication that these men wanted to entice him to their own camp; but on the contrary it is more than likely that they helped to make it possible for him to take that journey. "Providence provided me with money and a horse, and I went to see Mr. Griffith Jones, exhorting everybody on the way." After returning home he wrote some account of his visit to his brother:

I have been last Week in Caermarthenshire, for six days, where I met some of y[e] greatest in that County of my sentiments. If I shall not succeed here, Mr. Griffith Jones will help me to a School till I shall be provided for. He thought my being under age will be an objection, y[e] Canon is strict. I have been introduced to Lady Bevan, Lady of y[e] Town Member.[2] She gives herself entirely to doing good, distributing Welsh Bibles about, has several Charity Schools on her own foundation. I was in private Conversation with her for about five hours. . . . She has (they tell me) about £500 per annum at her own command—she has no children—and spends it mostly on charitable uses. I think she is y[e] finest Lady I ever saw in all Respects, twas a taste of Heaven to be with her; she made me a present of a very fine pocket Testament and encouraged me, whatever happens, to go on with what I am doing and that I should not want a friend. I am to Correspond with Mr. Jones and to be directed by him entirely. As I am too young unqualify'd and have no

[1] Rev. William Williams, a native of Llanfair-ar-y-bryn, Carmarthenshire, and closely related to William Williams of Pantycelyn, the hymn writer. He was the minister of Tredwstan from 1729 to 1762; he died at Brecon. He was a good scholar and an acceptable preacher.—G. M. R.

[2] Mrs. Bridget Bevan, the wife of Arthur Bevan, M.P. for Carmarthen. For many years she was Griffith Jones's patroness, and gave of her time and money to the Circulating Schools movement. She died in 1779.—G. M. R.

Title, I don't know whether tis prudent to offer yᵉ next
publick Ordination, for tis an affront to yᵉ Bishop to offer
ourselves under age unless he himself has first count-
enanc'd it.   If I had a Title in another Diocese I could
offer there.   Mr. Jones had taken a Nephew[1] of his to him
lately else he could have help'd me to one or two Churches
he has himself.

The portrait of Mrs. Bevan is painted in strong
colours; but it seems that she was a lady of notable beauty
and good sense, in addition to the excellency of her character.[2]   Were the above schools of hers the nucleus of
the Welsh Free Schools of Griffith Jones, which were
commenced a year afterwards?

It is sometimes said that those schools prepared the
way for the revival.   But it seems that the revival was
under way as early as they, and that it prepared the
country to welcome and to appreciate them.   Joshua
Thomas, the Baptist historian, was a native of Carmarthenshire, a keen observer, and old enough to remember
the circumstances of the time.   He fixes the beginning
of the revival in 1736, or before, and the commencement of the schools in 1737.   For that matter, Griffith
Jones himself testifies that the first of his schools was
opened in 1737.[3]   It is probable, therefore, that what he
promised to Harris was an English school under the
auspices of the S.P.C.K., if Madam Bevan's schools were
not also under his control.

By this time, Joseph Harris in London was being made
very uneasy by serious complaints that had come to his
ears regarding the irregular practices of his youngest

----

[1] David Jones, who was curate of Llan-llwch near Carmarthen,
1735-48, and vicar from 1748 onwards.—G. M. R.
[2] See *Life and Times of the Countess of Huntingdon*, Vol. I,
p. 454, note.
[3] See *Welsh Piety*, Vol. I.   Address to the Reader.

brother. Both he and Thomas, the other brother, wrote sharp letters to Trevecka at the beginning of this summer. But neither their reasonings nor their threats made any difference. Howell wrote to his brother, Joseph:

> I hope you'll forbear your endeavours to quench my zeal, for I hope tis impossible when I demonstrate so clearly tis no blind one. I consult some of ye Wisest of People how to regulate, and if you should read as much Divinity as you do Mathematicks I would ask your advice too. But Religion is not a speculative knowledge. Consider what brought this zeal to me,—twas not study'd or premeditated by me. I am only lead by an inward Principle: and did you taste—as I hope you will —what I do, you would not wonder how I have been able to go thro' so much. God never furnishes us with Weapons but expects we should fight, and to tell you my private Thoughts, whatever may become of me, till God alters my Thought, I am resolv'd to do all ye Good I can, tho' I ruin—if you call it ruin—my self by it. . . . Charge me with one imprudent step, speaking with an eye to Eternity. But as to this World, if God is God He'll rule. Let ye People be ever so unquiet as long as I never offended any Clergyman, or any other, or broke any Law, I am no more concern'd to hear their threats than to hear a fly. I should tremble to hear a holy man reprimand me, but Drunkards etc. have not ye keeping of ye Door to Christ's Vineyard. I apply to Him and all his servants . . . tis not fear of Disappointments etc. shall frighten me.

In another letter he recalls how Joseph, too, was derided at the start of his career, because of the uncommon bent of his genius:

> You acted as you thought best, although you had less to say of what you did than I have. Why cannot I have the same liberty to follow my conscience? I took not this work up of myself, it grew upon me so that I cannot now rest unless I am doing some good to others. . . . You may

observe something of a Particular Providence in some of
ye Latter scenes of my Life.   Was not that unaccountable I
should be disappointed of ye Hampshire School, which
you know was not lost by any wrong steps of mine? . . .
And was it not as strange I should lose Talgarth School,
which was not lost by any ill Conduct?   But did it not
directly come as a means to prevent my going from hence
to my doing farther good here?   Have I not been entirely
guided by your Direction?   Only in this one Point I must
differ with you, not that I think it a Rule for others to do
ye same, nor for me when this zeal ceases, but now I should
disobey an Immediate Call should I not privately teach y^e
Ignorant tho' I neglect not to read my Classicks as long as
I can. . . . I can't, tho' I was to be mouther'd, entirely give
it over.   I am sure that God that prompts me to it—which
I am positive of as all that consider seriously must be by y^e
uncommon Blessing that attends it—will not leave me un-
provided for.

Tho' I should leave all to follow such a Work, I know
my enemies shall have no room to Insult, for those that
Honour Him He'll Honour.   I am very confident that God
will never leave me tho' all ye World should, and that
He'll either take me to Him or provide for me while I am
ready to embrace ye first opportunity that offers for a
settl'd Life.

I have been with Mr. Griffith Jones last Week, . . .   As I
was not of age they would not directly advise me tho' it
should be prudent if I could get in, but rather to stay for
it if it be not on some emergent occasion ye Canons re-
quire—and our Bishop is strict too—to have a Certificate
from under ye Minister's Hand that we are full 23, which
as ye Ordination is 15th August and we must bring in our
Papers a month before, I shall want 6 or 7 Months of, but
if I had a Title—but none wants a curate in these Parts—I
should have offer'd, and Mr. Jones said if I should fail he'd
help to a School there, but that would put me off for 3
years farther, for ye neighbouring Clergy must know me
for 3 years ere they'll sign my Testimonial.   So that I think
I must stay here till I am of age.   In ye meantime to see

for a Title which I believe Madam Bevan may in ye Diocese of Llandaff help me to, which will entitle me to be ordain'd there, and with good Recommendation to ye Bishop we shall be ordain'd in Private. Thus you see I have endeavour'd to let you know ye Truth, and that my zeal does not carry me beyond Solid Reason and as much as I can I neglect not all proper Means towards my future settlement.

He began corresponding with the patriarch of Llanddowror without delay. At the end of June he wrote to him in the following words:

Were my Power and Zeal of ye same Latitude not one of ye Sons of Adam should be lost in ignorance. . . . Tho' it is my most ardent Desire, if God thought me worthy, of being an Instrument to do some good in ye World, the Honour of such a service and ye Gratitude I am in extraordinary manner under to my dear Redeemer for bringing me back when I had blindly gone to ye brink of Destruction, and ye Continual Joys I—an ungrateful Wretch—have daily shower'd on me, are Reasons sufficiently with me, His Spirit guiding and assisting me, to run ye largest Race and ye greatest Risques for His Glory. . . . As I know our Time is uncertain, so I can't omit doing present Good, . . . even to qualify myself in Order to have farther Power of doing good hereafter. So, being not of age, unqualify'd, and having no Certainty of a Title, and as possibly I might be objected against, I think it prudent not to offer for orders this Ordination. Ye Work has so expanded itself that I can't spare so much Time to myself if I should only Confirm those that are, I hope, already converted without aiming to carry it farther, as I am sent for to several Places. And I find as my Zeal is extraordinary, so is ye Blessing that attends my endeavours in some Places uncommon. I have had a Letter apiece from my two Brothers, which are according to my Expectation very severe, and I fear I shall be sent for to London if kind Providence does not interpose. Pray let me not want ye favour of your advice, for I'll be directed by you, nor shall I take any new steps without Consulting you, . . . for you are in my Eyes my Master's Steward, and I am one of ye Day Labourers. . . . I am in hopes of receiving His particular Commands thro' your mouth. . . . As what I am doing is of great Moment, and I am Young and ignorant, I crave to be recommended to ye Prayers of all God's Children in that Country, which is ye Petition of many of our Brethren in these Parts. . . . There are a great many, I hope, that have taken root, and many others that I hope will grow, . . . but much more in numbers are our Enemies and back-sliders, and great is ye Malice of ye adversary.

As may be seen from the above passage, the work held its ground wonderfully, in spite of all opposition. The darkest hour comes just before the dawn. When the leaders of the people were leagued against him, lo, out of their very midst came some to succour and protect him. Mrs. Parry, of Tal-y-llyn, we believe, led the way in this good work. She invited him to her house to read, and we are not at all sure but that it was there that the first Methodist society was established. We do not gather that she herself joined the new movement; probably she was in some perplexity as to what she should do, and thus her conduct was not always consistent. She would frown upon and show much displeasure towards Harris at times; but it was soon understood that she was un-willing for others to do so. As a result, the revival met with fewer obstacles in the parish of Llangasty than in any other part of the country. The result of this, in turn, says Harris, was that the professors of religion nurtured there were of a poorer quality than in any other place. Like Orpah, almost all of them went back.

Another lady, named Madam Phillips,[1] lived in the

---

[1] Theophilus Jones, in his *History of Breckonshire* mentions a charity bequeathed to the parish of Llanfihangel Tal-y-llyn by a Mrs. Mary Phillips.—G. M. R.

C

parish of Llanfihangel. She, too, had heard of the stir amongst the people and, imitating her younger neighbour, invited Harris to her house, and lent the influence of her name and her position to support the revival. As we revere the names and memory of those faithful women who ministered to our Saviour in the days of His flesh, it is fitting that we should remember, with respect, these sisters who nurtured His cause in its defenceless-ness and weakness. The action of these two women put a hook in the nose of the oppressor, and subdued to some extent his arrogance.

DISAPPOINTMENT AND LOSS
(July-September 1736)

SOME time in July, Harris received an affectionate and encouraging letter from Llanddowror. It seems that Mr. Jones, after reconsidering the matter, was inclined to urge him to seek Orders at the first opportunity, which he did. We have a glimpse of the history of these interesting days in a long letter which he sent in reply to Griffith Jones's letter.

Trevecka, July 31, 1736.

I should not have deny'd myself ye Pleasure of answering yours sooner, but that I have been continually employ'd in our Master's service ever since I rec'd yours, so intent that I could not spare so much time. I am yet ye more busy being apprehensive if ye Omnipotent does not miraculously stand for His weak Instrument, as my steps are more narrowly inspected to, ye little Liberty I have will be taken from me. I have been so powerfully set upon of late on all sides that Prudence could not decide what steps to take. But still, fear of man could not prevail against ye powerful chains of Love. Gratitude to my Saviour, ye effect of whose Intercession I daily feel, made me still look, ye same way, tho' I was put to consider and stand sometimes, that all Christ's servants that know me have occasion hitherto to turn their Prayers for me to Praises, and I hope God will never leave me so that I shall make any of those to grieve whom once I have been ye occasion of Joy unto. Tho' opposition and Crosses look us rough in ye face, yet when they are gone I find we are thereby drawn a step nearer to Christ, and we must consequently rejoyce. . . .

67

I have, according to your advice, gone about to see what Interest I had with ye Clergy here, and I found 'em all exceeding Kind. Five grave Responsible Ministers sign'd my Testimonial freely and a sixth—an old wealthy rich Gentleman—was pleas'd to recommend me to ye Bishop, being not able to certify for 3 years. A neighbouring Justice of ye Peace likewise stood my Friend and help'd to a real Title, all which unexpected Favours did raise my Hope to a high Pitch that God stood my Friend and that nothing could stand before me. But that my Patience might be excercised, after all these fair Promises I found his Lordship,[1] when I waited upon him with my Papers, so prejudicing preposses'd against me that as soon as he saw my Name in ye Top of my Testimonial he had not Patience to see who sign'd it, but with an offended Look gave me a severe check for what I had done and strict orders for ye future to betake myself to my studies, to obey my Superiors. And as he had such a Set of very good Clergy there was no need of such Proceedings, that I must entirely desist. He was so far from asking me my Reasons that he gave me no room to offer 'em.

Is free disinterested zeal for Christ's Glory so Hideous a Mark that we must watch against such at ye Door ere they come in? . . . But since they like ye earth so well let 'em take it, if they give me leave to drudge, they should receive ye Honour and Worldly Profits. . . . Shall I neglect doing present Good to follow private studies? I know not how short my Time is, and Zeal—that Heavenly Gift—is a fire sooner put out by negligence than by Opposition. Did the World seriously consider ye wonderful Reformation so generally wrought, especially in Young Persons, even those that only study ye present Benefit of Mankind would countenance such a Work. Those that are conversant in Scripture must own there must be a finger of God in it, and therefore not to be obstructed. But since I had things so well drawn up, and notwithstanding met such Testament, I utterly despair of ever having publick Authority

[1] Nicholas Claggett, Bishop of St. David's from 1732 to 1742, when he was translated to Exeter.—G. M. R.

to serve Mankind from this Bishop. And if I had it in our Church it should be so limited within Meshes of Parishes, etc., that it is contrary to ye Spirit I am acted by. My Desires are general, without any Limits. I rather admire those that tolerate me to sow seed in all Places you see ground apt to receive. I think I have already done as much, if not more good—if I had been permitted to water 'em that are converted—than I could from ye Pulpit in an age in one Parish. Nor have I yet any Qualification for publick service, my Gift being all Zeal attended with a Wonderfull success to ye familiar Discourses I have.

There are some very good Christians to consult with in common Cases, but few that have any uncommon Desires, their Reasons savouring something to me of the mire are, to suspend my zeal, etc., which stuck close to me too for some time after I was reprimanded by his Lordship, whose pretended objection was nonage. Yet, as there is a Prejudice in his Breast that seems to me to be irreconcilable to such Practices with his Reasons for 'em, and such a steady Resolution in me to go on notwithstanding all, it made me fall to ye safest side, to suspect myself. Then, flesh and Blood waiting ye opportunity strongly came in with these Reasons, viz., Shall I think myself wiser or better than all these my opponents, and how did I hereafter propose to live,—that my proceeding was contrary to Law and so sinful; and being so taken up with Divinity that I could not spare time enough for studying ye Learned Languages to prepare myself for Orders, and that my present Conduct was entirely new, having no precedent, being not authoriz'd by Law, even as tho' I had dissented from ye Establish'd Church. With these Reasons—which were not very slight ones—was I carry'd to hesitate whether I should proceed or not; and upon this Cowardly Submission to Flesh and Blood I found my zeal had left me. I could not speak to ye People with greater effect than any other Person.

That was attended with such Fear and Confusion that I fell to ye Throne of Grace with some guilt and some confidence as to having not hearken'd so much to carnal Reason as to ye Divine Command of obeying Superiors. And such did I find my Longings for that zeal I once had that I resign'd ye World and begg'd that Spirit whose Joys I had formerly tasted, for my Portion, whose Dictates I was resolv'd to follow for ye Future, wishing I was capable of serving Jesus Christ effectually. But such as I was I begg'd God to take me to His service, looking on myself no farther at my own disposal, and this was done in a stream of Tears and a Heavenly Frame. I was ye more earnest for ye Renovation of these sweet Blessings I privately so often enjoyed in my addresses to Heaven, having accidentally met some old Christians that once had tasted those Joys but were now deserted. I then resolv'd to go on and so went privately as before to Visit my Friends and to aim at enlarging ye Borders. Presently I found a Return to my Petition as well in meeting an extraordinary success even where I did least expect, and ye restoring of my sinking spirits to their former Frame. Then I could answer all ye objections that seem'd before so unanswerable, viz. that what I am doing is not what I ever contriv'd. . . . I would not neglect ye benefit of one Soul, much less so than to read all ye Books in ye Universe. If I am to go farther to ye Field, I believe I shall have Farther Assistance. Y^e zeal of some Young Persons in these Parts would make any one run ye risque to carry on such a Work.

Thus I have endeavour'd particularly to state my Case with ye several Combats of Flesh and spirit, and you being ye only Person whose Council I am resolv'd to follow, I hope you'll seriously Digest ye several Particulars as it is a Case of our Master's and not mine—for I only being an Instrument meet to be made use of. When you have ye freest communion with God, then pray think of me, that I might not want Prudence to act, and courage to fight; and ye more Ghostly your advice will be ye better, for I am not for dallying with Earthly Toys while Heaven is so full in my view. If some run ye hazard of their Lives for Honour, Pleasure and Worldly Gain, to ye shame of Christians be it spoken, if Christ has no servants in this Lukewarm age that shall be ready to Sacrifice themselves in His cause. O! how can we look to Him with one eye and to filthy Lucre with ye other? O! that my Portion was in this World to be quite spent in His service, and let ye World call me an Enthusiast, etc. Thro' His Merits I know I shall one day have an occasion to rejoyce with ye rest of His servants. . . .

I blush to see my Tediousness and uncorrectness. I always write what comes up sincerely, being resolv'd to have nothing to do with Criticks. . . . I just now rec'd in my Brother's ye good effect of your Friend's Intercession; he is mitigated, but as he is a stranger to zeal, so I can expect no encouragement from such as lay too great a Stress on Moral Duties. . . . Mr. Jones of Cwmyoe desir'd to be remember'd to you, and desir'd to know if you had any Intentions to see this Country soon.

On the back of one of his letters to his brother, Harris wrote an account of his experience after the Lord had restored his soul after the captivity referred to above. We set before the reader a few sentences as an example of what he wrote: "Oh! Send me where Thou wilt; I obey. I am Thine; manage me as Thou wilt. Lo! Here is a hand ready to write, a tongue to speak, legs to carry me—speak but ye Word. Oh! This Thy own free gift—as if embracing Him, loving, longing, admiring, praising, melting sick for Love. How can I bear having such sensible Proofs of the Intercession, etc. Oh! Jesus, to hear Thee reproached and say nothing. Let me have ye guidance of Thy Spirit; let me not go till Thou commandest, nor fear; when I am call'd make me to go; rule me, guide me and assist me. . . . Whatever Thou dost, take not these signs of Thy love away, else I shall be ye most miserable. . . . I'll leave all to follow Thee. Oh! I fear to lose this my only chance. I find others have and complain. Oh! Have pity on Jehosophat Jones. Oh! Remember Thy mercies of old, restore him. . . .

Oh! Keep all those converted by me, Thy instrument, from receding. Pity —— as one who has done much for me—now not with self-ends but as a Sister.[1] Pity Mother and my Brethren. Oh! Let me have this Honour of doing something to show my gratefulness. Oh! Let me be setting forth Thy Praise continually to men, Tears in streams, Joys unconceivable, to gain which for one hour it is worth ye Labour of one thousand years. . . . N.B. I had not these when I desisted from ye work for God. Rejoicing I am young that I may do much good, for on account of doing good I am willing to stay here, but otherwise years are tedious. Depend always on God in all things, for He gives me such an extraordinary stream of words on all occasions with ye unconverted, with ye converted, with ye ignorant and ye wise, with all opinions—and can't God when I appear before ye great Personages. Oh! What a gift had I with my neighbours tonight, so that ye most could bear reading and praying and singing for two hours, and ye rest for four hours."

He spent more than a half of the month of August in Carmarthenshire again. He was in Abergwili at the time of the ordination—with what object we do not know. He stayed mostly in Laugharne and Llanddowror. Many times during the years to come he refers to something which happened during this journey. It is probable that he did not fully understand its importance at the time. Until now he was continually in full assurance of the heavenly favour, and was never troubled with doubts and anxiety with regard to his own personal condition, whatever might be true of his activities as an exhorter. In vain the devil had tried to shift him from his stronghold through the persecution of enemies and the opposition of his relatives. But now, through the

[1] Mrs. Parry, probably.—G. M. R.

instrumentality of religious brethren whom he highly
regarded, the enemy had some measure of success in
bringing his experience down to the level of that which
was common in religious people at that time. An elderly
gentleman, named Mr. Dalton,[1] lived at Llanelli, a member of Griffith Jones's congregation. It seems that he was
a good man, a leader in the religious life of his locality,
and in Christ before Howell Harris had been born. But
he could not understand and had no sympathy with the
young awakener's strange animation and spirit, and now
he took it upon himself to advise him, and to lead him
to a more reasonable outlook and a more regular course.
He succeeded only too well; at least, he sowed seeds
which bore fruit in time, as may be gathered from the
following extracts from the later diaries. ''Now, through
associating with the world, I lost much of the simplicity
and sweet communion with God which I had when I was
despised by all men. By learning from them to make use
of human wisdom, and through Mr. Dalton's warning
me to be wary—that Satan could disguise himself as an
angel of light—the thought entered my mind that I had
been deceived, and thus I began to fear the work of the
Spirit on me. And because I was not under a healthy
ministry, and would not be led by the Spirit, I fell back
into working for life. Thus, though I still went forwards,
religion began to become a burden to me, and a slavish
fear began to trouble me, after I had been made as brass
in the face of all my enemies for nearly two years, before
I lost my simplicity. I fell under the power of unbelief;

[1] Edward Dalton, the 5th son of James Dalton, a barrister-at-
law, and Joyce Vaughan, of Trimsaran and Llanelli. His
brother, John Dalton, lived at Clog-y-frân near Llanddowror.
He and his brother were friendly with Griffith Jones, and staunch
supporters of the S.P.C.K. Edward was a toll-collector at
Llanelli. He died in 1761, aged 81; he was 56 years of age in
1736—not so elderly! He was with Howell Harris at Abergwili
when he first applied for ordination.—G. M. R.

I opposed faith as being presumptuous, and I embraced unbelief as humility. . . . Carnal reason all but ruined me. I lost my assurance by listening to Mr. Dalton who called it fanaticism, the work of the devil. I lost my first love—when I could not let anybody alone without telling him of his wretchedness, and when there was such power among us, that I was often on my feet all night for three nights in succession, and unable to desist. He advised me not to be so zealous; that God never asks such a thing of us. I soon yielded, not knowing that it was flesh and blood that loved that doctrine until the Lord left me. And when I asked Him why, He showed me it was because I had taken counsel with flesh and blood—that He had called me to toil day and night, to be a witness against all those who are idle in the vineyard. I lost my testimony by listening to those who called it spiritual pride, and in consequence I was in bondage for three years."

It is difficult not to be surprised that Harris should accept advice which savoured so much "of the mire," as he says. But it is probable that Griffith Jones agreed to some extent with Mr. Dalton's advice, and that he would have been glad, after Harris's application for Orders had been refused, to find an easy way to prevent him from itinerating. To that end they persuaded him that his present mode of living was not honourable; that he ought to do something to earn his living; and urged him to set up a school at Trevecka. "My submitting to Mr. Griffith Jones cost me three years of uncertainty through giving up my own opinion for that of someone else. If I had followed his advice and not gone about, probably thousands of people who now seek the Saviour would be yet in their sins." According to some accounts, the golden period of his life came to an end about this time. Doubtless he had equally exalted experiences after this (and especially on his way home on this occasion), but they did not last long. Likewise the same awful power often accompanied his ministry, but neither the exalted experiences nor the power were present with the same regularity as formerly. After coming within sight of the Promised Land, as it were, he turned back to the wilderness for years. From now on he spent much of his time in fighting his fears, and the corruption of his own heart; and the struggle was very hard until he learnt once again [in the words of William Williams of Pantycelyn] "to hand over all his battles to Him Who is glorious in power."

It is clear that these friends from Carmarthenshire only partly succeeded in their purpose. Although Harris's zeal cooled somewhat and he was tied to a worldly calling, he did not give up the work of exhorting as far as he could. If Heaven permitted him to lose much of his personal comfort, it took good care that he did not lose as much, if any, of his usefulness. Indeed it is likely that his present loss was nothing but Heaven's way of preparing him for the fulness that was to come. At the appointed time the slave was exalted from the prison-house to be a prince, eminently fitted to serve the Lord's people in their difficulties. Soon after this the societies began to be founded. Here was new work for him, and he had been prepared for it in a remarkable way. His early experiences had made him unique, but now he was made like unto his brethren. And as confused emotions had seethed within him night and day, he had become well versed in all the phases of the spiritual pilgrimage, and able to sympathise with, and to guide and to succour the pilgrims. As Williams of Pantycelyn sang in his Elegy[1] to him:

[1] The first two verses were translated by Edward Morgan, Syston—see *Life and Times of H. Harris*, p. 294—G. M. R.

Come and hear him now describing
  Man's foul heart—so prone to sin;
Tracing every inward turning
  Full of error, found within,
And disclosing many secrets
  To the righteous on the way,
While enliv'ning death's cold region
  With the glorious Gospel ray.

Come and hear him now expounding
  Heaven's free redeeming grace;
Loudly praising the Redeemer
  Of our poor apostate race:
Lo! He causes many a pilgrim,
  Sore oppressed with fear and grief,
To depart in joyous freedom
  From the bonds of unbelief.

He supports the arms that languish,
  And gives courage to the faint;
He sustains them with his doctrine,
  Heeding to their souls' complaint:
Glowing words, profound and earnest,
  Temper'd in the flame's caress;
Light to lead the weary pilgrim
  Safely through the wilderness.

Though the experience of the golden period was so
splendid, he had need, it seems, of further and different
experiences to render him capable of fulfilling such a
ministry, and to turn a Boanerges into a Barnabas. At
times he himself saw a new meaning in it all. Up to
now he had been a babe at the breast, a child on his
Heavenly Father's lap, extremely happy himself, it is
true, but at the same time of remarkably little use to his
Father or anybody else. The grievous vicissitudes he
now went through were but a necessary training, teaching him how to walk and giving him understanding.

His friendship with the Nonconformists lasted throughout these months. He says that his love was now free
and illimitable towards them and everybody else, and
whenever he refers to the history of this period he says

that he testified publicly throughout these months against the prejudice that existed in the Established Church towards Nonconformity. After attending the Communion service in Talgarth on the last Sunday in September, he says: "I prayed again, crying for him [Joseph], the vicar, all that are to communicate and that all may be meet partakers. Praying for above half an hour in yͤ Pew, I had such enlargements that I resolved to speak to yͤ Bishop to ask leave to feed Christ's Church, and if he should object on account of Languages etc. I would bring arguments enough to withstand, and that I should dissent."[1]

[1] *I.e.* join the dissenters.—G. M. R.

THE RISE OF THE SOCIETIES
(September-December 1736)

As has already been indicated, Harris had now been persuaded that itinerating and going from house to house was inconsistent with the Gospel, and that he should take up some employment to support himself. Teaching was the work most congenial to his nature; and as every other door was closed to him, he opened a school on his own responsibility at Trevecka about the middle of September. When Griffith Jones heard of this he promised him every support, and asked for further information in order to understand the situation. Here is a portion of his answer:

Oct. 8th, 1736.

I now confine myself entirely to my School which increases every day so that I have been obliged to take one to assist me to teach ye Welsh beginners in order to my having more time to instruct ye grown Persons. We have now 37, whereof 16 learn Welsh entirely, and I believe in three weeks time we shall have many more, servants, etc. Some have ye Spirit not only to undergo ye Scandal, lose their Time, incur ye Displeasure of some Friends, but likewise to go thro' other hardships as they have no Provision laid up and being at a Distance, and excessive Poor, they will be obliged—and some are resolv'd thereon—to sell some of their Necessaries. But others have not that spirit which notwithstanding seem inclin'd to learn but being able to surmount these disadvantages must remain still in Ignorance, if kind Providence does not Interpose. Y^e Integrity of my meaning and ye Truth of ye Case gives me assurance in ye stating of it before you, having had so many Tokens

78

of your Love for Christ. . . . My own Labours I am ready to give as being ye least I can do for my Saviour, and I am only concern'd that I know not how to dispose of many things I have that I might convert Earth to Heaven. Poverty does not frighten me, ye Necessaries of Life are easily acquir'd; let me only in some Measure be able to answer my Friends I am dependent upon. But what to do for Lodging, Provision and Books for my Indigent fellow Creatures? There seems to be something very enchanting in Riches, and I can't learn how Religion and Charity came to be separated; to understand really and fully that we are servants and Stewards is a harder Lesson than most People think. . . . We pray in Welsh morning and evening, and we have opportunity to give instruction on Saturdays. Next week we are to have a music teacher[1] to teach us to sing Psalms. I have distributed all the books according to your orders. We are beginning to set up private societies. I have only been six nights at home since I came from you. I trust they are taking root, but heads of poor families are scared of poverty.

This is the first plain reference to the societies that we have. It is difficult to say where Harris got his idea of them. His allusion to them in his letter comes in as naturally as if they had been a subject of discussion between him and Griffith Jones. Religious societies had been attached to the Established Church for many years. They were once very flourishing, but by now their glory had departed to a great extent. In 1739, when he first read Dr. Woodward's book,[2] which gives a history of their foundation and their activities, Harris states that he knew nothing of them when he founded the Welsh

[1] John Games, probably, the precentor of Talgarth church.— G. M. R.

[2] *An Account of the Religious Societies*, etc., first published in 1697; the 4th Ed. (enlarged) was published in 1712, the year of Dr. Woodward's death. Dr. D. E. Jenkins published an edition in 1935 (Liverpool: Hugh Evans & Sons), with an excellent introduction.—G. M. R.

societies. He evidently came to know something of them
quite soon. We understand that the Nonconformists,
too, held church meetings to instruct their people in
biblical knowledge, and to prepare them for coming to
the Lord's Table. Doubtless he also by now knew of
their methods, as he had a good deal of fellowship with
them, especially the Baptists. If he was imitating anyone at all, it is, possibly, their plan which he was following and perfecting. As the societies became more
numerous and began to attract attention, we find him
about six months later drawing up a petition to the ecclesiastical authorities, humbly requesting their permission
for the petitioners to meet with one another "to read, to
talk together about the state of their souls, to show the
results of what they learnt by self-examination, and to
ground the ignorant in the principles of religion," etc.
One of his reasons for asking that the request should be
granted was that similar permission had been granted in
similar circumstances within the Church at an earlier
date, in London and in other places. Another reason
was that many were leaving the Church and joining the
dissenters because this privilege of meeting together to
discuss the sermons they had heard, was enjoyed by the
Nonconformists.

But whatever its origin, the idea commended itself to
Harris's religious instinct. The scattered saints of the
district must be gathered together for edification, and
particularly for discipline. "That is the purpose of our
societies," he once said, "and to this end I was called,
and through the power of grace I will set up such discipline that no hypocrite will be able to bear it." This
discipline went beyond outward behaviour to the inner
experience of each member. As Dr. Lewis Edwards used
to say, the Methodist revival gave great prominence to
the place of experience in religion. For this reason the

fellowship was very soon christened *y Seiat Brofiad*.[1] In this respect no doubt the societies were something new in the religious history of the Principality.

While he was engaged in writing the above letter to Griffith Jones, a message came to Harris calling him suddenly to Talgarth. The schoolmaster had left the place, and now the school was offered to him. He writes to Griffith Jones:

> While I was writing this I was sent for abruptly to Talgarth by ye Disposers of that School, and ye Schoolmaster being gone away they offer'd me ye School, which in reality is only a School House—which I have Gratis where I am— and £2 Charity and possibly their favour too I may have by going there as 'tis their own Proposal—which perhaps I should forfeit should I continue where I am—for doubtless they would set up somebody there and then he not having sufficient encouragement by reason of my School they would suppress my School. Of ye other side if I should go there I believe I should not teach Welsh there and if I should—that being a large, debauch'd and idle Place—I question whether grown Persons should not be corrupted there, and I should lose ye only advantage I had, viz., of instructing them all in Welsh, explaining some of ye Principles of Religion, etc. It being a Mile from here I could not have ye Assistance from my Neighbour Women I have now to teach ye Beginners, etc., in order to have time for Instructing. Here is a private, Sober Place, Convenient for Lodging, etc., and there are many here already lodged, which being little Children some, and others with their Relations, I must lose. I shall be there under ye Inspection of ye Minister, and if I digress from the old beaten Rules I shall be called to an Account, and upon a Call to your Country to teach, etc. I should not leave that School, which is not ye Case here. So that I can't express how I am

[1] *I.e.* "experience society, or meeting," the main feature of which was the relating of religious experience. Members gave their testimony and were frequently examined.—G. M. R.

constrain'd by arguments on both sides which I have not Prudence enough to Judge which is Heaviest. . . . How did I know what my Master's Pleasure is, that am I most ready to obey. I hope you'll digest Impartially these Arguments and let me immediately have your Answer.

Before the end of the month he writes as follows: "I hope to get a hundred scholars. In the afternoon, as a rule, I could not rest; but after school and secret prayer I went to Garthbrengi. There, in consultation with my friends. They were in favour of my going to Talgarth. All things, spiritual and temporal, seem to be in my favour. Readiness to sell all that I have to give to the poor. The old zeal stronger than ever. Oh! Golden times! Oh! How sweet is life. It is Heaven." But by now, such "songs of praises" only alternated with "heavy groanings." In a page of his diary relating to these weeks he writes in a minor key. "When I received Mr. Jones' letter I could not find within me any of the spirit I once had. On Saturday night I went to Talgarth with a heavy heart, fearing that I would have to go there to keep school. But contrary to my expectation, I found the vicar was partial towards me, and I was lifted up to praise. At Trallong I was dull and sleepy. On Sunday morning I went to the church. I was asked to read in public, but I refused because of fear. In the churchyard I did not feel any compulsion in my spirit, but rather a spirit of fear. I attempted to speak without the Divine Commission, and I was humbled. Learning not to speak when not called; if I do, I shall do no good. I prayed in public before dinner at Aberbrân, but I was afraid to read; I departed dreading that I had offended God. On Monday in Talgarth with the Parson I lost all my zeal. I preached at home; no peace but opposition; but in Tal-y-bont I was greatly enlarged and melted in the public prayer. After this I went with friends to sing

Psalms. Tuesday, in school. I love my work dearly."

The following month he accepted the offer made by the governors of Talgarth school. "Things began to smile upon me once again. Talgarth school was offered to me, and in November, the night before I took it over, in the garden, I could hardly contain myself because of the working of my soul within me. I can never give anybody any idea of it—fearful lest God did not want me to go to Talgarth to teach." He worked harder than ever during this time. "I exhorted in school among my pupils, and I went secretly to houses in the night-time to read. Because I still read, and no one took any notice of my gift of speech, which I now exercised. They thought that everything was in the book, and that I prayed from the book, because I kept it before my eyes, seeing no harm in this at the time. This, together with calling my work exhorting, not preaching, was a means of blinding the eyes of my opposers. A door was opened for me to speak and to pray through a man who went about teaching people to sing Psalms. The people met for that purpose; and when he finished I would begin to exhort. During that winter I went with him to many parishes, and this was the origin of many permanent societies. I would go four or five miles distant from school, returning home about midnight—almost sleeping on the stiles along my way. I look upon it now (1739) with astonishment. Large numbers of young people gathered round me at the school, but their convictions were very slight, and many fell away for a time afterwards. Their love was only for me, and their reformation but outward."

Others besides Griffith Jones began to take an interest in him, and to help him. The following letter, from Samuel Rogers, a bookseller in Abergavenny, shows how talk about him spread abroad.

8 Nov., 1736.

It rejoices me that you do so much good in yᵉ World. My prayers shall not be wanting, as I hope yours will not for me. Whenever convenient opportunity permits me I will send some more Books gratis.

We have but one Welsh Bible; I shall send speedily for one or two more. The price is 5s. 6d., it cost us 5s. We have not one old one at present.

The reader may gather some idea of his activities towards the end of the year from the following quotations from his writings:

"December 9. How strange are the changes of this life! How desirous they are for me now, later raging just as fiercely against me, and then for me once again. When I think that the seed has been lost, lo! it is still growing everywhere unexpectedly, and the tares are scarcer every day. My understanding and my ideas become ever clearer. I find myself not in the least disturbed when they mock me, but I love being praised."

"December 19 (Sabbath). I was made to give and dedicate myself completely to God."

"December 20. I had lost the desire and the zeal for going to places given over to public sinning on Sundays, etc., but now I feel them again. After I had renewed the Covenant on Sunday, my zeal was restored. I deserved that God should withdraw His grace from me because I am so ungrateful, even while receiving from Him such exceptional powers, not given to others, *i.e.* sinners turned so quickly while listening to me. . . . Poor Mother! I see such blindness following worldliness, and the danger of keeping the heart from God while making a profession. How obstinately blind!—exposing me all the time, contradicting, envying, lying, etc. Thus, crosses within and without. . . . Disheartened because of the hindrances: but I shall go forward humbly, sincerely, and carefully—convinced that all these things are but to prove me. Daniel might as well give up praying, and the young men bow before the idol through fear of the fire, as for me to give up the work because of the clergy."

"December 22. Oh! That I could be as industrious, humble, and thankful as ever a man could be; because no one ever had greater reasons for being so. Who, until about two years ago, was so despised? and who now so honoured? Power and work falls upon me so that I can hardly attend to them. I was very weak for a long time limping along on my crutches, but now full of power and zeal. After losing my first zeal I regained it with greater warmth. I resolve to go to Bwlch, where I saw sin abounding, as it does everywhere. Oh! Christ, where are Thy servants?"

"December 28. I exhorted and prayed for about five hours; and wonderful authority accompanied my words. I now possess the same attitude of spirit as I previously had; but not so constantly now as then. Oh! How thankful and busy I ought to be when God turns, not one or two, but hundreds, through my words, while others preach and would give much to be able to turn but one. Learning humility from William Herbert, who supposed himself not worthy to be called my brother. Oh! What am I compared with him?"

"December 30. Enemies—Mr. James, Llanfihangel, etc.—turn from being wolves to being lambs. God sends His very great blessings with my words. The converts stand, and they increase in numbers and in grace. I feed on Heavenly things, and yet I am weak and oppressed. The old gift of using similitudes returning again."

The following note is very interesting in the light of what we know of the latter part of his life: "December

28, 1736. Reading of Professor Francke.[1] Planning to build an alms-house (after first selling all that I have and marrying ——), and to receive into service, and instruct, teach, and superintend myself, all that would come there."

One night round about Christmas time he went with the music teacher to a place called Wernos in the upper part of the parish of Llandyfalle; and there, soon, was established the first permanent society—the true mother society. "God brought me to Wernos (I trust can say so without presumption), and I hope some permanent proofs of grace have appeared. This was the beginning, though we used to meet in Tal-y-llyn, and in our own parish, and the house of Madam Phillips in Llanfihangel before this. But nothing came of those meetings, for it is not likely that the great ones will have a hand in the work." In 1738 he says, "Societies which had everything in their favour disappeared, but God keeps these poor worthless things. He wonderfully raised up means of helping to feed poor children here, and in other places, drawing them for the most part with love." And in April 1745 he writes, "I went towards Wernos in the parish of Llandyfalle, the place where all this great work which has spread throughout Wales began, and where the first society was established more than eight years ago. Full of joy to find an open door still here, and to see my old hearers to whom the word was sent so many years ago. There was a great crowd there."

We understand that Wernos is a farmhouse, seven or eight miles below Builth, near the main road which

[1] August Herman Francke, minister of Glaucha and Professor of Divinity at the University of Halle, who established his Orphan Asylum in 1698, and his Children's School in 1695. The author refers, of course, to the religious-industrial settlement— the "Family"—which Harris established at Trevecka after his separation from his brethren in 1752.—G. M. R.

leads down the Wye valley; it stands between Erwood
and Boughrood stations on the old Cambrian line, but on
the other side of the river. It seems that at present there
is no Methodist cause within some miles of the place, and
the neighbourhood is not particularly "religious." But
no doubt the place will be hallowed to every Methodist
who comes to know of it; and possibly pilgrims to the
local Spas will choose to pay a visit to the home of the
"first Society."

IN SORE STRAITS

(January-April 1737)

THE first months of the year 1737 were among the most troubled for Howell Harris. Apart from fears concerning his own personal state, and his anxiety with regard to the legality of his work, both of which at times weighed heavily upon him like a "body of death," he now bore a heavy burden of other troubles. Having now passed from the period covered by the mainly illegible diaries, we can linger more with the details of his life. Perhaps we shall gain a better idea of the pressure on his spirit by looking at him in different connections.

I. *Between two tasks*

Harris was not a moderate man in anything. Whatsoever his hand found to do, he did with all his might. He now proposed to serve the school in the daytime, and to exhort throughout the length and breadth of the whole district during most of the night hours. He threw himself into both tasks with the intensity that was so characteristic of him. But his physical frame could not stand the strain and he craved for rest. He would come to school in the morning with his body wellnigh spent with fatigue, and his mind sluggish and unready to deal with the children and their lessons. What constitution could stand this for any length of time? "What a miracle!" he writes. "I kept vigil for six successive nights till three o'clock in the morning, but I am still healthy. I did not strip my clothes but on every other night . . . I prayed for strength to withstand sleep, and contrary to the order of nature I wrote from eight o'clock in the evening till seven o'clock in the morning, and that quite clearly. . . . Only two hours sleep tonight. . . . To Wernos, but I slept whilst praying on the pathway. I was wonderfully aroused by the accidental coming of three sisters that way. I now do as much as I can day and night. . . . Working in school till past four, praying with the scholars till near five. Then to Trewalkin to see sick friends; then to Llan-gors: there till four; home after six. No bed. A great cross for mother, but I had patience to bear it. . . . No bed last night, good for nothing today, 24 hours lost. . . . Knowing that I had a great work to do tonight, and that sleep would overtake me unless I had supernatural strength, on the way I prayed, and Oh! joy! sleep forsook me at Brecon, and it did not come near me till cock-crow. Home after six. Sleeping for two hours. To school, but was dull all day. I had better not keep vigil, I see, or else my health will be endangered. I could not eat today, and I slept in church during the service. I find a trembling in my flesh because of the lack of sleep. I should avoid extremes. . . . I am almost accustomed to four hours sleep. I am happy because it has been conquered to such an extent. Nothing remains to be subdued, unless it be eating and sleeping."

No one can serve two masters effectually. If he cleaves to the one, gradually he will come to hate the other. It is easy to guess which work would suffer in this case. The school began to lose ground. "The scholars mischievous, light-hearted, and careless, but I could not find a spirit to speak with them. I cannot give them counsel except when I am given the authority. . . . The scholars dwindling away very quickly. This caused me to ponder more and more deeply. . . . My efforts with my scholars very unsuccessful. They abuse me behind my back.

Ashamed to come to school near nine o'clock. Sad, beating my breast in shame. . . . The scholars now few in number—they have dwindled from 80 to 25. Happy because I was kind to the man who took his children from me to the other school. I prayed on behalf of the young schoolmaster who is giving up at Chancefield."

It is clear that the breach in connection with education in Talgarth had not been closed. Chancefield is the name of a farm near the town, and we gather from the parish registers that Mr. Williams, the minister of Tredwstan, lived there at the time.[1] Thus it is probable that the Nonconformists, for the most part, promoted the other school.[2] We shall have more to say of the young schoolmaster later on.

Between one thing and another Harris's school quickly deteriorated, and this affected his prospects and his family comfort. He writes: "Heard that I was to lose the school. My mother treated me harshly. In complete obedience to her I determined to stay at home tonight. I obeyed her command for conscience' sake, and I went to bed and had communion with God. . . . Heard time and again that I was to lose the school. Disheartened, without any idea what to do. No hope from man. Asking God to provide me with bread: I desire no more. Everybody hates me because I teach the children to fear God. . . . Giving up every hope for the school, and (shame to my weak faith) preparing for prison. Heard at home that there was a warrant out to send the scholars

[1] There is reason to doubt this statement. According to the Talgarth Registers, Elizabeth, the wife of William Williams of Chancefield, was buried in 1730; William Williams, "late of Chancefield," was buried in January 1739. This person was not W. W. the minister of Tredwstan; he was alive *circa* 1762.—G. M. R.

[2] It is now known that a department, or a branch, of the famous Llwyn-llwyd Academy was held for a time at Chancefield.—G. M. R.

who are of age to their service,[1] and that I am to leave
in May. So weak in body that I could hardly look up.
I fell upon my face on the floor and I cried to God, 'They
are tired of me here. Oh! Lord! where shall I go?'"

Inasmuch as the trouble concerning the school increased, his soul clung the more to the exhorting. "The
Parson charged me," he writes, "that I did not live
canonically. I told him that I obeyed him as Christ's
minister, but not for fear of losing the school. . . . The
school deteriorating; but in Cwm-hwnt I received a blessing to be ever remembered. I wish that someone could
have been there to commit to writing the new, beautiful
and powerful ideas that I spoke there. . . . Teaching
will not satisfy me, especially when I see so few coming
to school. My desires are without limit, but I wish I
could do as much as my strength could stand—exhorting
every night (if my body holds out), or at least every other
night; teaching all day; writing, reading, examining myself, etc. Oh! Thou God! who seest these words flowing from my pen, consider my cause. I leave all to Thee,
though I know not what to do. For Christ's sake I ask
for—and expect—more zeal, etc. Because I count as
nothing that which I have already done. Do not be far
from me, to comfort me. Oh! that I had nothing to do
but to be altogether in Thy service."

Sometimes, to his great relief, the old power came
down in strength, transfiguring everything, delivering
him out of his distress and causing him to dance for joy.
"Societies have been, and are being, established in many
places," he writes. "God started the work, and He will
bring it to completion. I am persecuted at home and
elsewhere; but when I have the least communion with
God, they become as easy as anything can be. What joy
I now experience because I have run into every danger

[1] By this he meant military service.—Pub.

for the sake of Christ. I have never yet been guilty of neglect because of fear. . . . One night it was exceptionally wet and very dark: I had promised to go to Cerrig Cadarn; and in private prayer I felt some inner compulsion in my soul to go through any weather in order to prove my love to Christ. So I went, and my soul was filled with such joy that I leapt on the way, although I was drenched to the skin. There about nine: exhorting and praying till two; to bed at cock-crow. That night was blessed, I trust, to the conviction and calling of Sarah Williams[1] and others. About the same time, when I first went to the Builth area—to Rhydwilym in Llanddewi'r-cwm—my mother and aunt wept bitterly, after hearing that I was going to be ill-treated by the rabble from the town; and I was weak and afraid. But St. Paul's words came to my mind, when he was entreated not to go to Jerusalem, 'What mean ye to weep and to break mine heart?' And with the words such incomparable and indescribable authority was poured into my heart that I could not be terrorised had there been a cannon in my way. I could almost fly, in haste to be in their midst. O free, free grace! What have I done to have this? Nothing. . . . To Bolgoed. No preparation. Leaning wholly on God. Receiving such ability and blessing that I wondered where the words came from—so weighty, so clear, so prolific, so appropriate. There for nearly nine hours, till broad daylight. No weariness. How sweet and easy everything is when He works with me. I feared that pride might arise in my heart, so extraordinary was the gift."

There was a time when, after such services as these, he

[1] The sister of John and William Williams; they lived in Erwood in the parish of Cerrig Cadarn. The brothers exhorted with the Methodists, and John published a collection of Welsh hymns. Sarah married Thomas James, a well-known Methodist exhorter, in 1742.—G. M. R.

felt that he had nothing more to do. His work was to disturb and awaken the country. But of late a new feeling had come into his heart—a fatherly care for the converts, and a conviction that he should make provision for their nurture and growth after he had begotten them in the Gospel. Success now caused him almost as much anxiety as failure. As the work spread, he himself could not meet the demands made upon him—especially while still in charge of the school. And where could he look for help? Formerly, he would express his greatest desire to the Lord in the words of Rachel to Jacob of old, "give me children, or else I die." But now he was like Manoah, who asked, "How shall we order the child, and how shall we do unto him?" Or, on many a day, more like Hagar in the wilderness, lifting up her voice and weeping because she could not bear to see the boy dying of want.

Almost without a conscious realisation, on his part or on theirs, of what was happening, some of his spiritual children began to help him. The first to do so, it seems, was our old friend Joseph Saunders. The blacksmith was a man of ordinary attainments, but he had been given grace to be faithful "in a very little." He had probably accompanied his friend Harris very often on his nightly journeys, before venturing out on his own. Harris writes, "January 5. I should not be anxious concerning my preparatory reading in order to fit myself for exhorting; because I have had many proofs of God's love towards me and Joseph, bringing zeal, and words, and reasons, and arguments, from where I know not. I wish I could write them down. . . . January 3. My friend Joseph received wonderful power from God at Felindre, where I could not do anything. . . . February 28. Hearing of the splendid effects of Joseph's success at Grwyne Fechan." The ingenuous blacksmith was a refuge and a defence to Methodism in its weakness, and his name deserves to be remembered and honoured in its annals.

Sometime during the year 1736 an abler man than the smith was apprehended through Harris's ministry. He was John Powell, a native of Abergwesyn in the north of Breconshire. Before very long he joined the Baptists, but Joshua Thomas suggests that he was in the habit of preaching before he was baptised, and it is certain that for some time he laboured with the Methodists.[1] Were it not that he suffered from a certain instability of temperament this man would have won for himself a special place in the religious history of his country. As it was, he was endowed with an exceptional gift for itinerant preaching; and Christmas Evans was loud in his praise of him, three-quarters of a century after his death, as one who in his brief day was a means of awakening many souls from the sleep of sin. On the first day of the year 1737 Harris writes of him: "I had much gladness from John Powell from beyond Builth. I saw in him great signs of God's Spirit, great humility, wisdom and love to Christ. I rejoiced in my spirit having seen him converted. (I found pride within me, in that I rejoice more in seeing people converted through me rather than by means of others—but less of this every day.) I never found anybody else of this man's spirit. His words run through me with authority, like a sword. He possessed much knowledge from his boyhood, but he received grace from God's Spirit through me."

Quite frequently there was sharp contention between the two. Powell professed and preached an experimental assurance of forgiveness and salvation before any of the leaders in the Welsh revival. When Harris went to London, and had been led by the English Methodists to

<hr />

[1] He was baptised at Olchon by the Rev. Jacob Rees of Pen-y-fai, *circa* 1739. He preached against infant baptism, thus causing much trouble to Harris and the leaders of Methodism in various parts of South Wales. He died in 1743.—G. M. R.

embrace the same doctrine, he writes: "Had a seal through reading Rev. xxi. 7. Oh! sweet day. I had this before in Llangasty Church of old: but through yielding to sin and carelessness, and being curbed by almost-Christians, and because it was not given through [a Scriptural] promise, I fell again into doubts. Oh! how dear John Powell of Abergwesyn is now, who was so despised by everybody because he had experienced things that none other of us had known." It seems that he inclined towards the Baptists almost from the beginning, for Harris hesitated to place him in charge of one of Griffith Jones's schools in October 1737, "for fear that would be a snare to him, if God was calling him to the Baptists." It is not known when, precisely, he left the Methodists. But the following note is found in the diary: "October 26, 1738. A friend who intends to separate,[1] desires my prayers for guidance. Oh! Lord, lead him to the place Thou willest, and me also to the sect, and in the way that Thou seest good."

Harris mentions others to whom he looked for help—William Llewelyn from beyond Brecon, William Phillip, and perhaps Evan Rice; but we hardly know anything of them. A girl named Mary Phillip also used to read to her neighbours with considerable unction.

But these helpers brought with them an element of danger. Would the people who threatened the Leader allow others less qualified than he to labour in the same way freely and in peace? The sky was red and gloomy. While the children were out playing, or at their dinner, the poor schoolmaster in his distress would be in the old church at Talgarth, bedewing the floor with his tears. "Evil is repaid me for good everywhere," he complains. "My steps are watched, and I am slandered to the utmost. All sorts of evil is generally told of me, and I am charged

---

[1] *I.e.* to join the Nonconformists.

with things quite unknown to me. They watch me now as if it were their task, and I dare not move lest I am harshly judged. On my way to Tal-y-llyn I heard a sermon preached against me. My words are satirized in the most malicious manner. Lying down on the floor groaning for a long time. No guilt, but pure sorrow. Thou seest how many fall away, and how numerous are my afflicters. My bosom friends turn against me—John Games, once a friend but now an open enemy, seeking how to destroy me, leading everybody to frivolity. All Talgarth now persecuting, and this everywhere, except by the few who are raised by God. Thinking of the London societies. I beseech Thee, if it be to Thy glory, that Thou wilt permit us to meet. Raise up some to protect us—for they have authority and learning, which we have not. Thou seest how they hold it against me as sin, that I try to persuade my fellow-creatures to come unto Thee. Full of reasons to make a petition, that we might have the privilege of a society."

"Applying Saul's case [1 Sam. xiii. 8] to myself. Great fears that I have run too quickly. This shattered all my plans. Must I leave all alone again? In great straits for guidance. The various warnings I had from the clergy, on one hand—many likely to go mad—and the success on the other hand. Almost determined to be quiet and not to go. . . . Threatened thus, so that I look on this as my last visit here. Last night I ventured as one about to lose everything, and likely to be imprisoned. The clergyman, Thomas, was very cruel. Thou art now my only shield in these oppressions, when all the clergy are against me. Oh! that I might hear of someone taking up the work. My soul in sore straits. Will I go to Wernos tonight or not? Is it illegal to draw souls to Thee? Place my tears in Thy bottle, that we might have good ministers. Determined to take all pains to understand the classical languages, so that I might be ordained to feed Thy flock. . . . I fell down for the fourth time —my knees are painful. Here I am with all that I possess at Thy feet. I will address Thee till my bones tire. See my mother's poverty, and the death of Mr. Griffith Jones.[1] Sin within frightens me and oppression without; first from persecutors, then from those at whose hands I deserved better things—false brethren, as in Tredwstan, etc."

It will be seen that the accounts of extraordinary services are only one side of the page. Harris often walked "in the midst of troubles." Although he was half willing to lose the school, he knew not at what moment the work of the societies would be hindered again, he himself and his co-workers thrown into the stocks, and the converts left as sheep without a shepherd. What would become of them? Where could they find sustenance? It is not surprising that his grief became intense.

There were not wanting, on both sides, friends who missed no opportunity of showing him easy ways of escaping from all his troubles. He had but to give up the exhorting, according to some, and apply himself diligently to the school work, living in submission to his superiors, and he would soon find that the latter—in their own good time—would give him legal authority to do all the good he desired without anyone having the power to hinder him. He had but to give up the school, according to others, and join the Nonconformists, and he would find himself free to cater as he chose for the needs of his flock, and secure at the same time the protection of the law for himself and them. In this connection we shall see another aspect of the pressure on his spirit at this time.

[1] He must have heard a rumour to this effect; Griffith Jones died in 1761.—G. M. R.

D

IN SORE STRAITS (*continued*)

II. *Between two folds*

WHILE he was fairly determined to continue exhorting, whatever might become of the school, Harris was often much perplexed as to the particular group with whom he should throw in his lot. He loved the Church of his fathers passionately, and this is accounted to him as un-righteousness by some. But it is difficult to see how loyalty to convictions can be a virtue in a Nonconformist if it be a fault in a Churchman. Yet, in spite of his love for his people, he was as far removed from being a bigot as anyone could be. I know that Methodist historians as well as others teach differently, but that is my view up to the present. I have read his writings from the beginning to the Watford Association, 1743, in a fairly detailed manner, and if there was a single one among the public figures of Wales at that time more truly broad-minded than Howell Harris, I would like to know of him.

During the first months of the year 1737, however, it became abundantly clear that he would have to sever his connection with the Church, or leave his work; and there were times when he himself could scarcely refrain from seeking some other abiding city. We are not told that he received any invitation to join the Independents at this juncture; this happened later on in his life. For all we know to the contrary, he remained on friendly terms with them. Whatever the explanation of the reference to the "false brethren of Tredwstan" at the end of the previous chapter, it seems that William Williams, the minister there, was a quiet man, having little to do with the awakening which was stirring the religious life of the district around him. He probably never gave it much support, neither did he put obstacles in its way. He is referred to respectfully in the diary, and by 1742 Harris writes of him, "I heard from Joseph that Mr. Williams, Tredwstan, is now 'preaching faith.' I rejoiced," etc.

But if the Independents of the district tended to be apathetic, the Baptists were very lively. They spread their own peculiar views with great zeal, and it appears that many of them were too fond of controversy. Since they were hyper-Calvinists, and possibly more ardent Nonconformists than the other denominations, they stood at the furthest extreme from the Established Church. And as extremes often tend to meet, it was to them, more than anyone, that Harris turned when the situation became menacing in his own Communion. We do not find, in his writings, that he felt any affection towards Phillip Morgan, the minister of Trosgoed; but William Herbert was very dear to him for a long time. Herbert was a man of delicate health, living much of his time as it were on the borders of the other world; and the solemn thoughts of eternity, as a rule, curbed all contention and controversy within him. It was this same seriousness, no doubt, that had a short time previously induced him, a man nearly forty years old, to begin preaching. He held fairly tenaciously to Baptist principles, because he himself was a proselyte; and he attempted, from the best of motives without doubt, to win his friend Harris over to the same persuasion. He succeeded in preparing the way for converting him to Calvinism, but he failed to make him a Baptist and Nonconformist. At the beginning of the year he felt he was losing his hold on him. Herbert and his brethren had expected that the converts of the revival would have turned their backs upon such an unworthy institution—in their judgment—as the Church of England, and the shadow of disappointment is seen in a long letter which Herbert sent to Harris remonstrating with him concerning the course he was taking. We quote here some of the more interesting parts of this letter.

Jan. 8th, 1736-7.

My Dear Brother,

I need not repeat to you how I rejoice at ye Work of ye Lord prospering so well in your Hand: may ye Lord continue ye success thereof. I know you are for carrying on ye Essence of Religion, not regarding much ye Circumstances of it. I know well you aim well herein; for some indeed lost ye Essencials of Religion whilst they strove about ye Circumstancials of it. Yet, what I am going to write is of great Weight with me, and I can't find in my Heart to Waive it, and take up another subject: and therefore I shall write my thoughts freely and impartially, as one that shortly must give Account. Now I shall put myself in your Place and deal with myself accordingly.

Have I been labouring and toiling Night and Day to reduce and reclaim those that were like Sheep going astray? Did not ye Lord bless my Endeavours so far as to prevail with a great many to become religious? Are they not become willing to Separate from ye prophane World?

Now, how Do I serve these? Do not I in effect tell them to continue where they were before, when I send 'em to such a publick house which is open to all Comers? Where they must need have ye same Company and Conversation they had before? Don't ye Scripture tell me that ye Christian is like a *Garden inclosed, a Spring shut up, a fountain sealed*? If so 'tis different from a Common field, where every Noisome Beast may come. [Then follows an illustration from the curing of scabby sheep and turning them afterwards to a field of healthy ones.]

Do not my Conscience tell me that I put my poor tractable Sheep under ye Care of such Shepherds that are Hirelings and care not for ye Sheep? . . . But you may tell me, that there are some faithful shepherds belonging to that Common I send 'em to; true, but not in that part of it I send my sheep to; however my Conscience tells me, these have only yᵉ Name of Shepherds; . . . Did I not endeavour to guide yᵉ Blind for a Time along a Right Way, and then left 'em to yᵉ Conduct of a Blind Leader? Should I not rather continue to be their Leader, as well as continue to be yᵉ Shepherd of my Sheep? Have not I recommended to many that were sick and diseas'd, *Physicians of no Value*? Job xiii. 4. Have not I all this while encouraged a Mixture of Clean and of unclean Beasts? Even plowing with an Ox and an Ass together, contrary to Deut. xxii. 10? Did I separate between yᵉ *Precious* and yᵉ *Vile*, as I ought to do according to Jer. xv. 19? Did I advise my Friends as Paul did his in 2 Cor. vi. 17, 18? Did I not press yᵉ Word of God upon them in some Particulars, and in effect tell 'em not to regard it in other things? Did I not exhort 'em in several Instances to serve God in a Way and Manner yᵉ word of God is a stranger to? Did I not herein go contrary to Is. viii. 20? Don't I use to praise, magnify, and extoll such Shepherds and physicians, which I have Cause to conclude by their fruit were never appointed by God to their offices? Don't they do what they do for their own Sakes and not for God nor souls' Sakes? Did I not recommend praying by a Book, which is now yᵉ fashion of Men, tho' yᵉ Word of God is wholly Silent about such a way of addressing God from yᵉ Beginning to yᵉ End?

We all know but part: however I think I ought not to go to please Men any farther than yᵉ Word of God doth allow me, or else I am not like to be as true and faithfull servant of Christ as I ought to.

May yᵉ Lord teach us both for yᵉ future to keep a Conscience void of Offence both towards God and Man. We shall soon be remov'd hence, let's be faithfull in a little. I can't enlarge now. If I have health and strength I intend to use farther freedom with my faithfull Brother. Yours,

WILLIAM HERBERT

The testimony borne by this letter to Harris at the

end of his first year's labour is extremely valuable; and in fact stronger than anything found in his own writings. According to Herbert, his purpose was to promote the essentials of religion, rather than its outward forms. He laboured night and day to attain it, and God blessed His endeavours by bringing large numbers to a profession of faith. It is certain too that he felt the force of the other considerations found in the letter. But against these we must set the influences of Griffith Jones of Llanddowror. We understand that he frowned on the Baptists. We know that he warned Harris at this time against associating himself with the Nonconformists. He was now a very sick man, and rumours reached Talgarth more than once that he had died.[1] This made it more difficult for Harris to go against his dying counsels. It is possible, too, that the wiser among the Breconshire clergymen saw the danger and folly of forcing Harris and his followers out of the Church, at any rate, they occasionally treated him more kindly now. We find him having dinner, etc., with one or other of them on several occasions, and he greatly praises the goodness of the Lord in changing enemies into doves. The influence of his upbringing, the occasional courtesies of some of the leading men, the solemn warnings of Griffith Jones, together with a desire to keep himself in an advantageous position for reaching the hearts of the common people, proved to be stronger than the reasonings and enticements of William Herbert. Early convictions won the day insofar as he was kept from forsaking the Church of his youth; but he was in great perplexity of spirit for many months. He once thought of trying to go to Pennsylvania, and a hundred times he thought and prayed that he might be taken out of the way, to Heaven. Perhaps the reader would like to have an occasional glimpse of him in his distress.

[1] See footnote, page 97.—G. M. R.

These rival influences that were contending within him were embodied in David Lloyd,[1] the parson of Llandyfalle, on the one hand, and William Herbert on the other. The available diary is very full of references to the last phases of the struggle, when the balance was beginning to tilt in favour of the Church.

"I am attacked by Nonconformists and Churchmen. Praying sincerely to be set on the right. The one and the other love in me that which is similar to themselves. Self is in us all, but God has some in every place. I was counselled by my minister not to forsake my own Church. It has been in my mind since the day of my conversion that I am likely to do more good here. I never have such communion with God in any other place. Pitying those who vex themselves concerning rites and ceremonies. Determined to be always ready to suffer for plain truth, rather than dark matters in dispute. . . . Publicly declaring at last that I was for the Church of England. Exalting her greatly at Wernos, with a quiet conscience. I love Nonconformists because they love Christ, and because their books and sermons are warm. I will not look on small things, lest they should obstruct me in great things, as they do with many."

"Sabbath. Having dinner with Mr. Lloyd. Praising the Book of Common Prayer. No hypocrisy in that, because I love it, and my conscience approves it. Running down the Nonconformists. My conscience accuses me that I did not act honestly enough after loving them up to the present, being cherished by them, and now consenting to judge them. I lied also in not relating pre-

[1] David Lloyd was instituted to the living of Llandyfalle, about four miles from Talgarth, in 1713. He also held the living of Cefn-llys, in Radnorshire. He died about October 1747. His translation of Dr. William King's *Discourse concerning the Inventions of Man in the Worship of God* into Welsh appeared *circa* 1740.—G. M. R.

cisely how Griffith Jones set me on guard against them. Mr. Lloyd urged me to debate with them, and he liked me for consenting to run them down. I fear him, lest he should corrupt my increasing zeal: he is of a persecuting temper against the Nonconformists. My conscience was accusing me for not defending them. Such great fear, that I had offended God, that I could not lie down. Very bitter repentence, to the brink of despair, all the next day."

"Uneasy because William Herbert threatens to write to Griffith Jones. I fear I am not wholly free from prejudice towards the Nonconformists, but I disapprove of them. Wonderfully particular in confirming all in our Church to stay within her. Towards Trosgoed. The Baptists charged me with favouring set-prayers, and for sending William Phillip to Carmarthenshire. I tried to persuade William Phillip that he could be an instrument in the Church of Christ. To the extent that I see the Nonconformists loyal to Christ, and better than we are, I will love them the more. I prayed most fervently on their behalf. I find that they desire to draw every good man to themselves, so that he should be of them more than of Christ. . . . How can I do something exceptional for Thee? I applied for orders to serve Thee, and I was rejected; and that which I now do is condemned as illegal. . . . The Parson uncommonly kind and friendly. He showed me John Games's letter, and I told him how I was opposing the Nonconformists. Some good talk: but I was softened with shame and sorrow for my hypocrisy. But I do love the Church of England from my heart."

"Fears because persecutors are kind. I find my blood beginning to boil against the Baptists. Finding fault with them: but although the charge is true, it lay as a heavy load on my spirit. In all our conversations there is more bitter fault-finding than honest praise. . . . I think, if I am guilty of slavish fears in recommending the Prayer Book, that I could equally charge myself with being guilty of seeking the praise of the Nonconformists, if I did not persist in exposing their rigidness and extremes as I do. I was in some danger of becoming prejudiced against all the principles of the Established Church, without examining them, as a result of looking at the evil lives of her professors and because they persecute me, one of the same persuasion as themselves. I should have accounted that to the sin that reigns within them; because I find that such goodness as is within me is persecuted by such evil as is in the Nonconformists too. Having examined both sides carefully, I came after praying, to think little of myself, and to become settled in my principles."

"On my way to the church I heard that I would be sent for to dispute with the Baptists. At first I was so full of this that my mind was in a turmoil in the church; but on reflection I found that I was for entering the dispute in order to win the parties to love one another. I determined to do as much good as I could to the Nonconformists. . . . Behold here Popery, behold there excesses; iniquities here in the Anglican Church, and there too much rigidity. Oh! Lord! where shall I go? I am tossed to and fro by people of different views. Behold me at Thy feet to be guided; place me where Thou wilt. . . . Pondering over the petition I had sent. On reflection, I never saw anything lacking in the Church of England, except these three things: 1. The right to meet together as a society to consult together with regard to matters of salvation and self-examination. 2. More pressing home from the Pulpit the necessity of re-birth, together with family and public instruction; looking into the life of every communicant; a reason for absence from the service to be heard by persons set aside for the task; public examination on Saturdays before receiving any to the Lord's Table; and having a monthly Sacrament. 3. More intimate relationship between the pastor and the flock."

"I told Mr. Lloyd that I was seeking to settle William Phillip and William Llewelyn in the Church. I censured Phillip Morgan, but praised Mr. Williams and William Herbert. Very zealous against the Baptists. Fearing that the old spirit is beginning to cast out the spirit of moderation. . . . The words of the Prayer Book have a great effect indeed on me. My prejudice has vanished, and I see it a splendid book. I fear that I am at fault in opposing the Nonconformists, who draw some from among us to themselves. Beseeching without prejudice that God would not give me rest day or night if I am mistaken in my opinion. . . . At Bolgoed. Extolling the Church, in order to escape persecution, I fear. I am afraid lest I should grieve the Spirit by so doing . . . Envy in my heart in hearing of William Herbert's success. O! vilest of men that I am!"

"The clergymen I feared most are now my best friends: Lloyd, Davies, James of Cathedin, Williams of Aberhamlach are now for keeping me in the country. Behold the promise of Psalm xxxvii. verified. . . . Fearing that I was at fault in extolling the Church. Fully persuaded that one way or the other—as ways—are nothing in the sight of God, but new creatures only. Greater desire for this spirit than ever. Confessing my jealousy of William Herbert. What a favour was this after being left to myself for so long a time, having been without communion with God for two days, although still receiving the help necessary for the work. I had no zeal in William Llewelyn's house, where I exalted the Church excessively, to the neglecting of other things. Great zeal in

the other house, where I made no mention of the Church
at all. I know not what to do. Lying for a long time
on my face on the floor of the Church, with the stench
of the dead in the dust, I pleaded fervently for more
knowledge of God. There are few that stand for Christ;
because of this I craved for a weapon in my hand to fight
on His behalf. I prayed that I might be instructed in
judgement. I had a feeling that all judgements governed
by humility, and in line with His word, are acceptable
through Christ. I believe that the way of the Church
of England is right, if the life corresponds. I made an
offer to William Herbert not to speak of any religion,
but only of faith and repentance. Seeing myself unworthy to wipe his boots."

"I nearly made an idol of all the Nonconformists because of the presence of some good men among them;
and I became prejudiced against the Church because of
the wickedness of her adherents. It is dangerous to talk
of or to read one side only. Hoping now to find a number of true servants of Christ in our Church, that we
might join together in private, to humble ourselves and
to give thanks. I am from my heart, with a quiet conscience for the Anglican Church. I tenderly prayed that
God would light a few candles in her. Lead Thou the
Papists, and us too, and all the Nonconformists to the
right path. I prayed on behalf of William Herbert and
all who have at heart the interests of Christ Jesus. I
determined to stay faithful to the Church: that is where
I am called. All souls are precious in God's sight. I
extolled the Church with such substantial reasons that
even the Nonconformists could not take offence, and so
I kept the spirit of love. I established every one in his
principles, and thereby safeguarded them from separ-
ating themselves because it seems to me that they should
not do so. Oh! God, have pity on the many thousands

of souls whom Thou seest completely neglected and ignorant. With Mr. Lloyd. He is harsh towards the Nonconformists, but approves the London societies. I am wholly of the same opinion. I have been mistaken long enough, but now I see differently. I rejoiced greatly to see him so encouraging to all good things."

"Oh! Lord! if I have done wrong in extolling the Church, convince me of it. I am ready to give up every opinion. Thee, Thee alone I seek. Have pity on the Church of which I am a member—the poor, troubled Church of England, which is rent in pieces by her sins and her ignorance. Oh! Jesus! are not all souls alike precious in Thy sight? Send lights into the midst of her. Let us go forward in our true endeavours to follow Thee. . . . I hear that I am to be fiercely persecuted by the Nonconformists. In the direst straits what to do. Seeing many turning back, for lack of shepherds I fear, and all in danger of growing cold. In doubt whether I did right in exalting the Church; but I feel a very great and genuine compassion for her—where so many myriads of souls are starving. My soul in sore straits, not knowing what to do. At last, I felt such compassion for her that I cried out, 'Let me be Anathema for the good of all the Church of England. Hear the groans and sighs of Thy poor servant. Behold, I am a worm. Oh! have pity, have pity on them. Let me be turned to destruction for their sakes, and send shepherds to care for them.' "

"William Herbert threatens to write to Madam Bevan against me. Discouraged because the Nonconformists persecute, and many grow cold. Hesitating as to whether I would go to Wernos or not. How I am straitened because Thy true servants persecute me. Bless them and help them. Forgive me for giving them cause to hate me; and if they are mistaken, forgive them too. Inasmuch as I myself was converted in this Church, and nurtured by her hitherto—as also are many others—and as her principles seem to me to be sound, forgive me if I was at fault in exalting her, in order to gain more freedom for myself, to instruct poor ignorant souls."

"My confession of my principles which brought the persecutions to an end, and seemed to pacify all, served but to provoke Thy servants the Nonconformists. And now, with no one here to feed Thy flock, and I myself without the remotest prospect of receiving Orders; and as their being persuaded to go to the chapels can only be followed by harmful effects, what shall I do? Oh! God! why cannot we all agree in the same work? If Thou dost not call me to it, then I will take on some other work without delay—digging or something. . . . To Wernos. Many accusations against me by William Herbert—that I make fun of immersion; that I prevent many (who used to come) from coming to the meeting; and that I, in order to escape persecution and to be freer from restraint, am exercising too much carnal wisdom, thus casting a blight on Nonconformity, and taking part with the persecutors; that I went beyond Brecon not as the apostle of Christ, but as that of Mr. Lloyd; and that he was afraid that God had withdrawn this blessing from me. I was furious; but I confessed every fault, and I told him of his faults too, and of my anxiety with regard to the poor converts. In great straits, as I saw that the work is not altogether successful; and that great and small are bitter against the Baptists, in spite of my sincere efforts towards unity. I found him meek and humble-minded: but standing for the Scriptures. Ready to kiss his feet. Then to Llandyfalle Church. Mr. Lloyd was very kind. Can I not hide my love for the Nonconformists and thus keep his support? Oh! God! remember my prayers, and help me between Tories and Nonconformists to walk in a straight path, looking unto Thee."

The above sentences, culled here and there from the diary, are but a few of the more striking expressions on the pros and cons of this matter. The citation of ten times the number would not serve any better to show the state of affairs. We see that Harris, and many of his converts, began to be drawn towards the Baptists about the end of the year 1736, and that this aroused the anger of the Churchmen towards him more than ever before, so that in the end he was forced to choose between the two parties. For better or for worse he succeeded in keeping most of his people from leaving the Church; but William Herbert and other of his friends were disappointed on that account, so that they did not hesitate to use very bitter words to him and of him, to his great sorrow.

Two years later, in recalling this trouble, he writes: "That which once inclined me to the Baptists was,— 1. My ignorance of other Christians, they seeming to be so good. When I came nearer to them I saw that they were but men, and afterwards I saw in others as much of the humble, gentle, sincere, Israelite-indeed spirit as I had seen in them. 2. My ignorance of the principles of religion. Thus, because I was unarmed, I was exposed to attack on all sides, and nothing but compassion for souls in this Church [Anglican] kept me from them, I believe. 3. The unruly, carnal lives and the preaching of our own ministers;—so many carnal men on my side; and Bunyan, Vavasor Powell, etc., on theirs. 4. A tender conscience fearing to give offence in anything. 5. Their constant pressure upon me and attempts to persuade me on every side. I see now that the basis of all their approaches to me was just this—to bring me across to them."

It is clear that compassion for the multitudes was the main reason that kept him from leaving the Church at this time—the same thing that many times kept him from giving up the work altogether. When he became discouraged because of the opposition of the world and the Church, and the corruption of his own heart, it was always the kindling of his compassion that caused him to take up the work once again. Whatever views are held today with regard to Harris's character and motives, readers of his diaries know that they are all erroneous if they do not emphasise, above everything, his compassion —"so great compassion." And that compassion was not only wonderfully strong but also equally wide in its scope. No one could escape from his warm-hearted nature. "Are not all souls alike precious in Thy sight?" he says in the passage quoted above; his writings abound with similar expressions. He felt that the ministry he had received from the Lord was meant for all, and especially for the lower classes, and for the indifferent, for "such as turn aside to their crooked ways"—without priest or presbyter to check them on their ungodly course. Many Nonconformists were extreme hyper-Calvinists. They held that God had ordained multitudes to perdition, and that it was futile to offer the Gospel to such people. Inevitably therefore the time came when their narrowness came into conflict with Harris's broad-mindedness; and an occasion soon arose which drew him into the morass of theological disputation. In this very connection the third element in his trials becomes evident.

IN SORE STRAITS (continued)

III. *Between two views*

IT is agreed that the majority of the scholars of the Established Church in those days, insofar as they had any theological views at all, held a mild form of Arminianism. Harris had been brought up in the atmosphere of that teaching, and the more faithful he was to it the further was he led from what is commonly known as the evangelical position. His own experience, during "the first year," pointed in a different direction; but now, these many months, he had slipped his moorings. He had not yet been drawn to the study of any system of theology, and his ideas were very confused. One night, at Wernos, whilst speaking against reprobation, he made a declaration of his beliefs. He laid all the blame on man's unbelief. Man, he said, ought to know that he is in a dangerous plight even here and now; and since he is to exist for ever he should prepare himself for a future state. All threats and promises should be adapted to the fears and the hopes that are within him by nature. Once he sees the danger, the instinct of self-preservation will urge him to seek for help—to use the means of grace, etc. Since the will is corrupt, reason will make the choice in its stead. If he believes in avenging torments on the other side, self-interest will compel him to prepare for that which lies beyond the grave. Then will come the struggle and—having been defeated in it—he will seek for aid: having received aid, thankfulness will follow, and from that thankfulness will be born love. Eventually he will dread to offend Him, who—as he understands

from experience—alone is his constant help—for he
cannot do anything of himself—and so he will seek to
please Him, to behold Him, and to enjoy Him. From
this comes a hatred of sin, although he cannot leave it,
any more than a man imprisoned in a dungeon. But
he can follow the example of the Prodigal Son, and prepare a place for the Blessed Helper through fasting, etc.

Here is his own account of his theological wanderings,
as he looks back on them after many years. "For a time
I endeavoured to convert myself and the people by
reasoning, without looking upon it as the work of the
Spirit. I fell into the error of exalting the power of man,
arguing that all men could repent and return. I lost
much of my earlier simplicity, by exercising human wisdom and listening to Mr. Dalton; and I began to doubt
and to fear the workings of the Spirit within me. I knew
but little concerning Christ, although I spoke much of
Him, and was deeply conscious of Him in my heart. My
inner teachings compelled me to confess that I could not
do anything of myself; however I spoke in this inconsistent manner for a long time. Although the Gospel was
within me, I was led by the principle of the law, because
I did not simply follow my inner teachings, but sermons,
books and my own carnal reason. For a short while
Christ left me too, even as He did the apostles of old."

The Churchmen of Breconshire were much pleased
with this teaching. "I hesitated when I understood that
the carnally minded clergymen were pleased that I was
calling Election the Doctrine of the Devil. . . . When I
denounced Election, many who formerly hated me began
to love me for this reason. This led me to examine why
they loved me; but yet I continued to proclaim that man
could turn himself, as otherwise my preaching was in
vain."

But the Baptists could not tolerate this teaching: they

were offended by it to such an extent that they sometimes broke out in open opposition to him during the service. "To Wernos. Much tender feeling there: but in speaking of Election I offended the Nonconformists, and a warm debate ensued; but God helped me. I made an open declaration of my opinion on the matter, against the view that God ordains men to perdition. A gift of utterance was given me; my bowels were melted so that I could humble myself to my opposers; and they were melted through this. Great joy because I had been thus reconciled with my enemies." It is clear that it was Calvinism, in its most extreme form, that was offered to his notice, and it is no wonder that he felt a strong repugnance for it.

Thus, while his reason and his Anglican friends drove him in one direction, his experience and his Nonconformist friends drew him in another. "Although experience always taught me that I could do nothing except it were given me; yet I was a strong Arminian, and at Wernos I debated with great zeal against those who held predestination. I withstood that Doctrine for a long time, and all the people and all the reasons in the world could not bring my proud stubborn heart to embrace it. I was taught the Doctrine of Election slowly, in stages. The seed of belief in it was sown when, quite early on, I became certain of the immutability of God. But the Doctrine did not develop for some time after that; and I, because of the darkness of my understanding, denied it and opposed it till it pleased God to instruct me further."

"Wednesday, March 30 [two years to the day when he first came under conviction], I went to the public service in church. I saw from the second lesson [John xvii.] that there is such a thing as Election, and I entertained humble hopes that I was one of the Elect. But, in spite of everything, Arminianism was still in my head, until, one day, when I was vehemently contending for man's power, saying, 'What is the good of preaching to him, if man cannot turn and repent?', a certain man appealed to my own personal experience, asking me how I felt in secret prayer. Did I not see myself so dead and lifeless that I could not free myself from that bondage, any more than I could fly, until the power came from Someone else—a power which I could not command but which was given according to the good pleasure of His will? I could not deny the truth of this. 'Then,' he said, 'would you be telling the truth if you confessed that you could not pray?' 'Yes, of course,' I answered. 'If so,' he said, 'why do you lie to the people—that they can believe and repent?' I was silenced, so that I could not use these expressions any longer, since my own experience condemned me. I saw how I had been caught in the devil's snare, by setting up my own wisdom instead of submitting myself to God's teaching. My intention was good, as I saw things—to anticipate laziness and spiritual inertia in my hearers."

"Some time after this, whenever I opened the Bible, my eyes seemed always to fall on John vi. 44. But such was the enmity of my carnal reason against the wisdom of God, that I would secretly blame Infinite Wisdom for setting it there, and I strove diligently to explain away its real meaning. At last, the devil became my teacher, whispering to me, that God drew everybody. This served pretty well until I read verse 37 of the same chapter. Then I was brought to believe Election in my heart; my wisdom yielded to the wisdom of God, and I confessed with my mouth unto salvation."

In this, and the two previous chapters, we see Harris cooling in his ardour towards the school, but warming to the work of exhorting; drawing away from the Baptists, but cleaving more to the Established Church: turning his back unwillingly on Arminianism, and half-embracing the Doctrine of Free Grace. That was his position about Easter 1737. There is no doubt that he was utterly conscientious in all this. He did not choose the easiest path. Although he remained in the Church of his fathers, he at the same time refused to give up his work on the orders of her princes; and he adopted and proclaimed views which they hated "with perfect hatred."

We give, as a conclusion to this chapter, a few extracts from the diaries, which could not conveniently be inserted into the foregoing narrative. They may well show more clearly certain aspects of Harris's life.

"In Abergavenny. Heard that I was a great Revivalist. I felt humble and thankful. Marvelling, revering, and praising God for this honour bestowed upon me. A view of His goodness in raising me up, me, who could boast nothing from ancestry, upbringing or natural gifts, but who am indeed the poorest of the people and the chief of sinners, as I have shown before in my confession —raising me to such a height of honour that my name is honoured by good folk exalting it, and by the wicked trampling it under foot. . . . In Buckland. Lord keep me from the rich, and from those who call themselves huntsmen. What scoffing I endured because I rebuked one for swearing, and what arguments against exhorting were pressed upon me! One of them thought that forgiveness could be obtained by confession and the reciting of the Lord's Prayer; and that they would give up sinning when they were dead. They threatened to write to my brother, that I would lose all preferments, that I would go mad, etc. I see no pleasure at all in their company. They swore continually, as if on purpose to annoy me, and all their conversation was about dogs. Any men-

tion of God they called preaching, and therefore threw
it aside at once. I find pleasure with none—indeed I
feel acutely uneasy in all company, except in that of
those who love Christ. . . . To the inn with Mr. Williams, Rhos [one of the Independents of Tredwstan]. I
stayed there in true sorrow of soul from twelve until
nearly three o'clock. I saw the horrible nature of sin.
Nothing but swearing, talking of dogs, etc. Rejoicing
that I need not be always in such company."

"Discouraged by the thought that I am so far from
being qualified to receive Orders. But, Lord, Thou
seest how things are. What time have I, day or night?
Wilt Thou not prepare for me such a place as will make
me more useful to Thee. I have nothing to lean upon
to justify myself but an uncommon blessing upon the
work. Let me not be without it—the only reward I
seek. . . . Oh! the goodness of God! When they obstruct me, He raises others to go forward, taking my will
for the action. I have done as much as I could, day and
night, for over a year. I believe that the foundation is
safe, because up to the present the building stands. . . .
When I gave everything away thoughtlessly to the poor,
and was reproved for it, —— unexpectedly gave me 27/-
during the week. Fearing to marry her for the sake of
her property. Great longing and fervent prayer for her
conversion. I was on my way to her; but at Trefeinon
and Llan-gors, becoming filled with zeal for my Master's
cause, I failed to visit —— as I had intended."

"What changes I have passed through during the past
month. When the school was broken up I was full of
fears because of the folly of friends and the malice of
enemies. These came to wean my heart from it, and to
show the uncertainty of all things. I humbled myself
and prayed: then the hatred of the enemies was turned
into great love. Learning from this to be quiet, and to

depend upon God's power in the hearts of our enemies as our sufficiency. How often have I seen oppressors being made doves, without any natural reason for it; so why should I fear? The purpose of these shocks is to strengthen my roots. . . . Praying with friends in the gate, as in the fields some time ago. My understanding is opened more through one prayer, than by reading or much conversation without divine help. I see many truths, some of which, I think, I understand well enough to preach on. This is no natural gift. I am full of observations, and although I cannot write them down, I rarely fail to remember them when I need them. Lord, Thou knowest that I believe I do more good by going about at night to exhort, than by reading privately at home. All knowledge comes from Thee; and as I have no time to read, I know Thou canst instil into my heart clearer and purer knowledge than I could ever suck from books. Therefore I will rather spend my leisure in prayer, leaving it to Thee to supply me with arms. Is this caused by laziness? When I read the Bible, I constantly discover something new in every verse. Such is my case that many of the Psalms are applicable to me. I find that in an extraordinary manner, ideas have already become clear in my mind which I subsequently discover in my reading."

"I see little humility within me. I often spoil my intentions to do good from the lack of this. We are prone to take the example of Luther—a fearless man— when our cause is not the same as his. When the people are inside the walls of a town, a battering-ram is essential; but in open battle such a weapon is useless. So it is now, I imagine; and from this root grow all the dissensions in our midst. If I were to see humility in the enemy's camp, and obstinacy in my own soldiers, I would suspect that Christ was against them. I see that it is from a lack of humility that I take the liberty to censure others, and, without considering the temperament of the person I speak to, I give my counsel not as a brother, or considering my own failings, but in a harsh, churlish, arrogant, perverse manner, which is never effective. The humble address succeeds best in the school of Christ, and impudence among the friends of Satan. . . . We ought to look into things carefully, especially if we see a good man among our opponents. I must not call him evil because he is against me; because it is possible that he has consulted with God, and has been encouraged to oppose me."

"Welsh and English hymns streaming out in a natural way. I rejoiced with the little birds as they sang, and I saw the ugliness of sin restraining us from enjoying these sweet things. I believe it is essential to advise people of a melancholy temperament to seek some form of diversion. . . . From Cerrig Cadarn to Erwood, I was full of fun—with me, the usual result of great success, I was rightly charged with frivolity. I was not put out but confessed my fault. Judging myself severely because of the extreme levity of my nature. My exhortations are stifled by my frivolity: but I will begin to be serious now. . . . I am afraid that it was pride that made me speak of my labours to Evan Rice, hoping that he would report them to my credit in Carmarthenshire. I nearly wrecked myself on the rock of pride once; and now again I am sailing on that same sea. In danger as the result of praise. Thankful for persecutions to keep the balance. . . . Reading Locke on fanaticism, I feared that it was pride that led me to reform. . . . Since Thou givest freely, I will not be content with an ordinary measure of grace. Make me as poor and as despised as Thou wilt; but give me spiritual wisdom, give me an unusual knowledge of Thyself."

"To Pwll-y-wrach, to see my sick friend, William Price. I was melted with the hopes he had of going to his Father. I sat by the fire reading, but I slept. When I awoke I found he was about to depart. I tried to pray, but I could not because of streams of tears. Then I saw him dying. For about an hour my face was washed by my streaming tears. My soul was so closely united to him that I could hardly leave the place. Great joy because the first I saw dying was so full of comfort; and because God had made me the instrument of his conversion. A few minutes before this he prayed with strong faith, full of consolation: he pleaded for a blessing and pardon for his parents, and when I asked him, if I could lift him up, he replied, 'Oh! You have lifted me—to Heaven'; and entreating our prayers he died peacefully. The thought of eternity made me resolve to redouble all my efforts; and the memory of the purity of his zeal, and his untiring diligence in self-examination, and in search-ing the Scriptures, brought anew a flood of tears. . . . To his funeral. Threatened, and accused of having caused his death. But I had communion with God, and looked upon myself as a king in the midst of the crowd. . . . Very fervent for my dissolution. Waiting in humility and hope that my Lord will not be long. A desire to see my friends once again to bid them farewell, beginning tonight. Praying for ——. My words do not avail, but Thou canst speak to her heart. Then I could die without seeing her—the only creature that has my affection. For my mother, with tears and compassion more than ever; and for my brothers in a most fervent manner. For the converts. Such compassion towards them that makes me almost willing to remain among them. . . . Hearing of a series of persecutions—public and private, general and particular. It is delightful to look at the waves from the rock, Christ."

"A heavy cross from my mother: she sought to persuade me not to go out to read. I suffered her surliness patiently. I prayed and she was wonderfully melted. Then to Wernos in peace. I heard at Tredwstan that Margaret of Maes-gwyn was going mad, and that she could not last much longer. My heart was nearly broke, and I was afraid to go on. I have never before, on any occasion been in such agony of soul. I could, from sheer misery, have thrown myself into the ditch and lain there for ever. Were it not for the assurance I had just had of the efficacy of prayer, I could hardly have walked my lonely path. Trembling with fear, my heart nearly breaking; but with no sense of guilt while looking to Heaven. I did not say a word to cause this, yet, in considering so many who are near to giving up in despair —Mary Perrot, Rebecka of Pwll-y-wrach, Priscilla Williams, and Margaret, John of Llan-gors, and the fanaticism of William Williams, I feared I had not been sent, and that it was sinful for me to go out without being ordained. Oh! God! if I am being deceived, Thou knowest my innocence. Oh! Lord! Oh! My Father, have pity on Margaret, Thy poor creature; let not our enemies triumph over us. . . . At last I received strength to surrender the matter to Him, and to go forward. Much of my burden was taken away, although my soul still seemed to be encased in lead. I feared it was not anxiety for the interests of Christ that caused my uneasiness: but a concern for my own name. To Maes-gwyn. I found Margaret fairly well, and I was kindly received where I expected insults. Great joy in her company. Then to Wernos."

"Burdened in spirit while thinking of how I should get on above Brecon. The doing of good through me is the greatest wonder, seeing that I am of such a cowardly spirit. Great comfort from Luke vi. 21, which was providentially recited to me by one of the girls in the course of her lesson. . . . Was it my idea to have Psalm-singing as an opening for holding a society meeting? No: no more than I intended going about at the beginning to read. In all probability we would not have been suffered to meet for a long time if God had not raised up men to sing. When I was anxious about what we should do after this, God raised up friends for me. . . . Good news today—the work succeeding in spite of vigorous resistance. It would be easier to read at home, and that would reconcile everybody; but I am encouraged by the success. . . . All my money has been given out for Christ, to buy books, etc. I have but one sixpenny piece left. Visiting the sick. I gave my last sixpence to Christ."

"I see two laws within me in all that I do; one seeking the praise of men, and the other hating it. How good is God—suffering some people to expose my defects. Great longing for the Sacrament: knowing that strength is to be obtained there. Sin is a burden, especially laziness. Lord, wast Thou brought before the court for my sake this night [Good Friday] and shall not I, too, suffer? Thou hast made me, but not to sin; help me to realise the purpose of my creation. I wish to spend my time in doing good; I feel I do this by exhorting, but I fear I do not by writing. Some people mock me, saying that to hear me once is enough—that I have always the same thing to say. I addressed the neighbours with a tender humility such as I had never known before, and they all wept. I understood and felt that I could not do anything without the aid of the Spirit. What should I do if He were to take away His Spirit from me, as He did from Jehosophat Jones?"

"It is seldom, if ever, that I feel an inclination to public prayer. Ashamed of going to Carmarthenshire, for fear they would ask me to pray. I determined to spend more of my time in private prayer—my only joy and comfort. I see that morality—as it is taught—tends to keep men from Christ as much as anything. I felt my own lack of power today more than ever. I see that grace is a free gift. This, and all that is good, comes from my Saviour's intercession. . . . Lord, Thou knowest that nothing can make me to hesitate, apart from doubts as to my commission. Oh! That I knew I have been authorised! . . . Is it not the finger of God that makes so many stubborn and intractable persecutors to submit to reproof, and to be so unmistakeably reformed, when the clergy and others could do nothing? Oh! I must remember, never to give up. I am fully persuaded that the work is of God."

ANSWERED PRAYERS
(May-August 1737)

WE come now to a remarkably interesting period in the life of Howell Harris. But, unfortunately, all his records for the twenty weeks or more following Easter 1737 are missing, with the exception of a brief account of one experience on an afternoon in June. Thus we have to do the best we can by drawing upon references found here and there in the later diaries or letters.

Harris fulfilled the apostolic command to be instant in prayer as faithfully as any man. Whatever his deficiencies, he prayed without ceasing. Prayer is interwoven with all his thoughts, and all his words, and all his activities. Almost all the contents of his writings during the first years are prayerful meditations. The few historical references we have are drawn along in the wake of his devotions. Of the blessings he most fervently craved, four may be especially noted, *viz.*:

1. To find an open door for the work; and men of position and character to protect him from his persecutors.

2. To have a personal friend for himself—a Jonathan to whom his soul could cleave.

3. To have awakened ministers to be lights in the Established Church.

4. To be led to a clearer and broader discernment of the deep things of God.

And now the appointed time drew near for his confidence to be rewarded by the granting of these blessings to him.

1. About the beginning of May every door seemed to be closed against him. Having forfeited the kindly interest of the Nonconformists because of his Churchmanship, and the tolerance of Churchmen because of his increasing interest in Calvinism, he felt that he was as the heathen, ostracised by all. But the darkest hour precedes the dawn. "About the month of May I began to 'speak publicly' at Wernos and other places, and I cast the book away. On Ascension Day, when the door was almost closed against my going about, the son and daughter of Mr. Williams of Skreen came to hear me, and to ask me to come and exhort there; and so I went. I was now about two years old. During those two years I was enabled to travel about two thousand five hundred miles on foot, at a moderate estimate. By now my preaching gifts had grown: and I began to talk a little of Christ, but still ignorantly enough." Mr. John Williams of Skreen was a gentleman of means and position—he had been the sheriff of Radnorshire the previous year—and doubtless his influence helped and protected the work for a while. One of his daughters was converted through Harris's ministry, and joined the society at Erwood, suffering the extreme contempt and hatred of her relations as a result. Seven years later she and Harris were joined together in holy matrimony. Never having felt the authority of the truth in his own conscience, his daughter's membership of the society caused Mr. Williams to frown upon the revival; but not before a more powerful protector than he had appeared, in the person of Mr. Marmaduke Gwynne of Garth.

The reader will remember the common tradition with regard to Mr. Gwynne's enmity at the beginning; his coming to one of the services with the intention of taking the preacher into custody; together with the way in which he himself was caught in the Gospel net. Perhaps this

is not wholly true. We gather, from one statement in
the diary, that it was at Skreen that Harris met Mr.
Gwynne for the first time in August 1737; and, surely.
it is hardly likely that a gentleman would have come to
the home of a magistrate of another county to interfere.
However that may be, he was won over, not only to give
his support to the new movement, but also to become a
simple and faithful disciple of Christ. He was a strong
pillar of the cause for years, and only the last day will
declare what service he rendered. When Harris's pocket
was empty, his purse was open; and when the petty gentry
and magistrates of the neighbouring counties raged, the
influence of the Squire of Garth brought them to heel
on many occasions.[1]

The door was opened wider and wider still for Harris.
Through the instrumentality of Mr. Gwynne and Mr.
James of Gilwern he was welcomed to upper Brecon-
shire; and a Mr. Prytherch, of the family of the famous
Rhys Prytherch,[2] led him to the Llandovery district. Mr.
Williams of Bolgoed and John Powell of Glyn had
already introduced him to the districts just north of
Brecon; and now he crossed the River Usk, going further
south. Friends from Pen-y-lan, Llanigon, led him to
Llowes and the borders of Radnorshire, and others from
Longtown brought him to Herefordshire. Many are un-
aware of the fact that he was invited to Pembrokeshire
in the summer of 1737. We do not know for certain
who invited him; we shall give our opinion on this matter
later on: but Griffith Jones of Llanddowror was the
obstacle in his going there. Mr. Jones was disturbed by
the action of a layman in taking upon himself the pre-

[1] Marmaduke Gwynne, in 1749, became Charles Wesley's
father-in-law; Sarah, C. W.'s wife, was one of six sisters.—
G. M. R.

[2] Rhys Prytherch (1620?-99), of Ystradwallter, near Llandovery,
a famous Nonconformist minister and teacher.—G. M. R.

rogatives which belonged to the clergy. "Mr. Griffith Jones was the first to make my itinerary ministry a case of conscience. From that time I was never entirely happy about it. But I was drawn on by the earnest entreaties of godly ministers, and the cries of the people; and not by any spark of my own zeal."

2. The reader will remember Harris's reflections, at the beginning of his career, on the value of friendship. He was naturally of a cheerful and sociable disposition; and he found his greatest joy in the company of a kindred soul. When, as the result of his conversion, he was thrown into complete isolation, neither constant prayer nor a sublime experience of communion with the Unseen could at all times or altogether extinguish his desire for companionship. It seems that his mother was a woman of harsh spirit and temperament. Natural affections often caused her to feel a certain amount of concern for him; but she could not, and she would not, sympathise at all with the aims and objectives of his new life. He had to seek outside his own home for the comforts of fellowship. We have recounted earlier his midweek walks from Tal-y-llyn to Trevecka, undertaken for the sole purpose of seeing the few persons who could to some degree sympathise with him; and how his soul was knit with Joseph Saunders, ordinary and uncultured as he was. Perhaps it was this propensity, rather than any intention of changing his single state, which led to his connections with Mrs. Parry of Tal-y-llyn. We know that this was so in the case of his next attachment, Mrs. James of Abergavenny.[1] He longed and prayed for someone of a like mind with himself to whom he could pour out his soul. And in the summer of 1737 he found him.

[1] Mrs. James, in 1741, became the wife of George Whitefield.— G. M. R.

His new friend's name was Howell Davies—the man who today is known as the Apostle of Pembrokeshire. It is rather difficult to say with any certainty from where he first came to Talgarth, or his exact reason for doing so. It is as Harris's assistant at the school, I believe, that we first become acquainted with him. We can give no account of his coming; but I offer a conjecture, in the absence of anything better. The reader should remember that this is only a conjecture and not an established fact. For some reason, a second school was opened at Talgarth (perhaps by the Nonconformists) during the previous spring, and a young man (presumably from Monmouthshire) came there to teach. He lodged with Mr. Williams, the minister of Tredwstan.[1] Many children went from the old school to the new one, causing some bad spirit on both sides; but Harris was moved to pray for his more successful rival. It was quite natural also that the latter should be interested in Harris, and that he should find himself, one day, listening to him exhorting. In this service a new world opened before his mind:

> "Earth receded from his sight
> Heaven opened, clear as light."

All things were made new to him that day, and the idea of running a school in opposition as it were to his greatest benefactor became immediately unthinkable. Indeed, for a while he felt that he could not even live apart from him. The two schools were merged in the warmth of the teachers' love for one another; and the younger of the two moved to Trevecka to take up his abode with his father in the Gospel.

In support of my theory, I could note:

i. That the other school and its schoolmaster are not mentioned after this.

[1] See footnote, p. 90.—G. M. R.

ii. That Davies was converted under Harris's ministry.

iii. That Edmund Jones of Pont-y-pool was early acquainted with the former.

iv. That Harris heard him preach for the first time in the churches of Llanhiledd and Blaenau Gwent [in Monmouthshire] at the beginning of 1741, when Davies was a curate to Griffith Jones, Llanddowror.[1]

But whatever may be said for or against the above, there can be no question as to the friendship between the two men, and their affectionate partnership with one another, until the older of the two was ejected from his post early in 1738. They delighted in sharing each other's innermost spiritual experiences and in dedicating their lives together to their Saviour during the closing months of that year. The younger of the two became so devotional in spirit that on some nights his friend was full of awe as he lay beside him in bed. When they had to part, Davies, at his friend's instigation, went to Llanddowror school. They met there from time to time, and in the summer of 1740 we find Harris praying that the Lord might open the way for his friend to be ordained. If his age, as generally reckoned, is correct,[2] he could hardly expect to be ordained sooner, as Bishop Claggett [of St. David's] was so punctilious. Dr. John Morgan Jones[3] is mistaken in sending Davies to Llys-y-frân [Pembrokeshire] at the beginning of that year; and Mr. Beriah Gwynfe Evans is still more mistaken in naming Davies

---

[1] In the Moravian Records once kept at their chapel in Haverfordwest, Howell Davies, it is stated, was "a native of Monmouthshire." His uncle, William Williams of Bolgoed in the parish of Llansbyddyd, is mentioned by Bennett in this chapter. W. W., possibly, was the brother of Howell Davies's mother.— G. M. R.

[2] Howell Davies died in 1770 aged 53; he was born therefore *circa* 1716-7 and would be about 23 years of age in 1740.— G. M. R.

[3] *Y Tadau Methodistaidd*, pp. 128-9.

E

as one of the men who laboured to prepare the way for
Howell Harris. Neither is it correct to set him up as
one who worked independently of his spiritual father at
the beginning. It was Harris who first sent him to
Llanddowror; and there is reason to believe that it was
Harris, in accordance with his belief that "all the salt
should not be put into one sack," who afterwards persuaded him to go from there and to settle in Pembrokeshire. We know that Harris incurred the bitter displeasure of Griffith Jones by taking his curate from him,
but Harris would not suffer anyone's favour to weigh
against what he considered to be for the good of ignorant
souls.

3. With the exception of the rector of Llanddowror
and the vicar of Cwm Iau, Harris up till now did not
know of one clergyman who had any living power in
his ministry. But now he became acquainted with three
more. One of them was the Rev. David Lewis, incumbent of Llansanffraid Cwmteuddwr, near the town of
Rhaeadr Gwy in Radnorshire. I am sorry to say that we
know little of him. But we do know that—very unlike
his brethren—he preached Evangelical Doctrine, basing
salvation on Free Grace rather than upon man's attainments. He died about four years after this. Another of
them was the Rev. Thomas Lewis, his son, curate of
Merthyr Cynog. He, too, preached the same doctrine as
his father in a lively and effectual manner; and very
soon his church became a centre for the converts of the
revival in the upper and middle districts of Breconshire, as Cwm Iau was at the other end of the county.
This brought upon him the wrath of his superiors, and
the societies were kept in constant suspense lest they
should lose him from their midst. Many times were days
of prayer and fasting kept on his behalf. In the end he
was forced to leave. As he was about to accept the curacy

of St. Harmon's in the northern confines, the curacy or living of Llan-ddew, near Brecon, was given him: and it is as Thomas Lewis of Llan-ddew, or Talach-ddu, that he is known to our historians. He was the fellow-labourer of the Methodist Fathers, and a foremost man in their Associations for many years.

The name of the third, the Rev. Daniel Rowland of Llangeitho, will be remembered as long as the people of Wales have a regard for religion and virtue. His history deserves to be recorded in detail, especially in a book dealing with the origins of Welsh Calvinistic Methodism. But since our task is to gather up the fragments which have been neglected by our historians, and since we have nothing new to relate of Mr. Rowland, our remarks must be very brief. He was born [at Nantcwnlle], near Llangeitho, in the year 1713. He was the son of the incumbent of that parish, and he too from the beginning was intended for the ministry. He was ordained priest at a somewhat early age.[1] According to Robert Jones of Rhos-lan, he was a curate in Carmarthenshire for a while.[2] Then he returned to Cardiganshire: and for many years he was curate to his elder brother, who held several livings in the vicinity of their home. For a time he was wholly irreligious, but he was convicted, it is said, while hearing Griffith Jones of Llanddowror preaching in the church at Llanddewibrefi. Soon afterwards, he too began to preach with extraordinary power. The most magnificent ministry of the Welsh

[1] He received deacon's orders in 1734 and was priested in 1735. —G. M. R.

[2] *Drych yr Amseroedd*, p. 69. In a letter to Mrs. James of Abergavenny in 1742 Rowland refers to his "communicants at Ystrad Ffin" and he informs his friend, "I am suffered to be no longer at Ystrad Ffin." It seems that he ministered in that little church for a season, whether as a curate or as an itinerant, we know not.—G. M. R.

pulpit then began, and it lasted for over half a century to be the mighty power of God unto salvation to thousands of souls.

Some insist that Rowland had begun to itinerate before Harris.[1] Since his journeyings had extended as far as the counties of Carmarthenshire and Breconshire in 1737, it is argued that he must have commenced in the vicinity of his home long before this. It is certain that Harris had heard nothing of him before this summer. It is almost equally certain that Griffith Jones also knew nothing of him, otherwise Harris would have heard of him through this source. The ear of the man who had prayed so much for revival would be sensitive enough to hear, and his pen ready enough to write of these things, if he had heard of them. If we can accept Robert Jones's statement, old ecclesiastical associations could explain Rowland's coming to Carmarthenshire so very soon after he had started upon his career as a Revivalist. However that may be, it is Harris's constant testimony that he was the first in Wales to go about the country exhorting. It is difficult to say how soon afterwards Rowland began. If he had started in 1735, would not Claggett have refused to ordain him in the August of that year? And if he had started in 1736, would not news of it have crossed the mountain to Abergwesyn, and would not Harris have heard of it through John Powell? We gather, therefore, that he began to travel beyond the confines of his allotted sphere of labour some time towards the end of the year 1736.

It is useless now to conjecture what led him to the neighbourhood of Brecon at the end of the summer of 1737, about the time when his Lordship of St. David's

[1] William Williams, Pantycelyn, for instance, in his elegy to Daniel Rowland states that it was Rowland who "first started out."—G. M. R.

customarily visited his diocese. Is it possible that Rowland was already numbered with the transgressors, and that he had been called to appear before the courts to be reprimanded.[1] Or, was he perhaps at the time acquainted with the parson serving in the parish church of Defynnog —who, it seems, was more serious minded than most of his brethren? Whatever the explanation, it was in that church that Harris first met him at the time already noted.[2] Amazed by his extraordinary gifts, and the power and authority with which he spoke, Harris's heart burned with love towards God and the preacher. The friendship formed at this time lasted for about thirteen years. This was followed by a period of grievous coldness, again of some thirteen years' duration. Subsequently the two friends were reunited in the bonds of peace which remained unbroken, and which never will be broken any more.[3] They were the two leading figures of the revival in Wales: and their history, to all intents and purposes, is the history of Welsh Methodism in its first phase.

4. Harris profited much from his acquaintance with the above-mentioned men. He was brought to a clearer understanding of the truths of the Gospel. We cannot do better than to tell the story in his own words: "Little by little my eyes were opened to know the mystery of the Gospel. The Lord kept me from reading the mere letter of Scripture, from increasing merely in head knowledge. But as I grow inwardly, I gradually come to see and to understand this verse and that. I received the Gospel not from man, nor from a book, but from God:

[1] The ecclesiastical court records are now kept in the National Library of Wales; there is no record of any disciplinary action against Rowland at this time.—G. M. R.

[2] The actual date is 13 August 1737.—G. M. R.

[3] The two men separated during the disruption in the movement in 1750—see the Epilogue at the end of this book.—G. M. R.

that which I experienced, proved, and felt, and saw, and heard of the Word of Life, that also will I proclaim."

But although he wrote thus, he often generously confesses that it was by means of this or that person—irrespective of denomination—that the Lord opened his eyes. "About Christmastide, 1736, I began to think of Christ, as the result of brother William Herbert telling me that he was about to die, and that none but Christ could then support him. Before this I had placed the emphasis on man's work. When grace kept sin in chains I thought it was man himself who did it, through carefulness, etc. At Merthyr [Cynog], in 1737, I was first enlightened to see the Doctrine of Free Grace: although my experience had shown me from the beginning that I could do nothing in my own power. Was it not Providence that brought me there? Mr. Thomas Lewis preached from John i. 12. It showed me clearly that I had received Christ. (It is one thing to possess faith; it is quite another thing to exercise it; it is one thing to be in the Covenant, it is another thing to know it.) After this I found much sweetness and strength through hearing his father preach from Rev. iii. 20. I had previously fallen a victim to doubts, and as a consequence under the dominion of sin, because of my ignorance. But now, I came to see the difference between unbelief and humility, and between faith and presumption. But at Gwenddwr, in that same year, my eyes were opened to the light when I heard Mr. Rowland preaching on Prov. viii. 32. He was the means whereby I was brought to the knowledge of the truth about Christ. It was in that same year, also, I think, that I came across a book called *The Sincere Convert*,[1] which was used to turn me from duties and frames, to

---

[1] By Thomas Shepard; a second edition of a translation into Welsh of this work had been published in 1727.—G. M. R.

depend only upon Christ. I had previously come to see the Doctrine of Election, but now for a while I fell into believing in Reprobation; but I was weaned from the latter by reading 1 Tim. ii. 4; 2 Peter ii. 9; and Ezek. xxxiii. 11." In addition to the above, he refers also to sermons on the two Covenants which he had heard at Llanddowror, to Doolittle's book on the Sacrament, together with other books, as means which were blessed to him about this time to lead him further into the light.

He used to say sometimes, after this, that two faiths and two conversions were necessary: the first from the law, and the second from the Gospel; one to believe in the Father, and the other in the Son; one to wound and slay, the other to revive and heal; one to reveal sin, the other to conquer it; one to work fear, the other love. No man was ever more ready to acknowledge his ignorance, and to wonder at God's choice of so unfit an instrument to further His work in the world. "All this time I was given sufficient matter and appropriate headings wherever I chanced to speak; and when I had used this material everywhere I was given fresh matter and new light. The ways of Providence were indeed wonderful in sending forth such a youngster in age, maturity, knowledge, experience—one so uncommonly inclined by nature to levity, lust for pleasure, laziness and pride! (to all of which, nothing could provide a stronger temptation, than my very position). How He raised up friends for me! When I was in the greatest straits, I was never finally overwhelmed. Oh! If the World but knew how ignorant and worthless I am—I am speaking honestly and deliberately—this would certainly be a permanent monument against all Free-willers, Deists, Arians, Arminians and Atheists: and it would make everybody glorify the work and the wondrous effects of free grace. Truly, this is the only wholesome preaching."

Towards the end of June the tone of his experience strikes a low note. He complains that God had withdrawn His smiles from him—smiles which he had formerly received so freely: and he deemed that his laziness, or his dependence on feelings, was the cause of it all. But it would be difficult to find anyone else who would regard him as being guilty of laziness. After dwelling so long with his complaints about himself it is a relief to turn to the testimony of others to him. Mr. Rees Davies of Abergavenny wrote to him in August, begging him to postpone his ordination, lest that should curtail the scope of his usefulness, and restrict him within the confines of the parochial sphere. He writes:

> So many Souls will Lose ye Benefit of your Labours and pious efforts for the Good of perishing Souls. So I humbly Conceive 'tis for ye best Interest of poor Mortals for you to defer it for Some Time: . . . Go on, Good Sir, with your Flaming Zeal for your great Master's honour and Glory in this Lower World. Your Reward, you know, is Exceeding Great, far above our finite Conceptions in this our Weak State. 'Tis a true observation that Zeal is a Qualification Necessary in Christ's disciples, which helps in ye Excercise of every Grace and in ye performance of every Duty. You know, Sir, that Christ Commands us to be zealous.

He then goes on to lament the general lukewarmness of Christians of all denominations.

The same month a certain Howell Jones, a schoolmaster, sent him a Welsh letter declaring his longing "for a blessing and success upon your work, your talks and Evangelical Reasonings, and upon your hearers; who, I hear, are very numerous. Although many are against your going on in the unusual way you take; yet, since you are a free agent, those people should not be surprised that the Candlestick has been removed from its place to give a brighter light in the thick darkness which has spread into, and over precious souls, who are content to live and die in their present condition, etc., etc."

The change in Harris's views effected a change in his preaching. His ministry became more Scriptural than it was before. He preached more and more in the following months on Zaccheus, Rev. iii. 20, and portions of the last chapter of St. Luke. Besides this, he also changed his method of carrying on the work. Prior to this he had worked cautiously and secretly, at least after persecution had begun. But now, according to his own view, the work and the worker became more *public*. The letters of William Herbert and the Abergavenny people show that the *effects* of the work were already quite well known. But the seed had been sown at night, or in secret, and in a comparatively confined sphere. It would be wrong to talk of thousands, or even hundreds, congregating to hear him before this time. He laboured furtively, travelling on foot, more often than not under cover of darkness. But soon after this the cords were lengthened. He travelled boldly in the daytime, and he no longer confined himself to the limits of a parish or even a county. A messenger would come from afar with a horse to fetch him, and sometimes he would be away from home for a full week, leaving the school, presumably, in the charge of Howell Davies. Nothing but his connection with the school stood between him now and being a free man. This, together with the powerful reinforcement which came through the ministry of Mr. Rowland and others, caused the work to succeed in a wonderful manner from now on. Certain whole districts became religious; especially those parts of the parishes of Cerrig Cadarn and Llandyfalle, around Wernos, Llannerch Goedlan and Erwood. The day of small things, in the story of the revival, had come to an end.

THE WELSH SCHOOLS

(September-December 1737)

THE story of Harris's visit to Skreen, and the conversion
of one of Mr. Williams's daughters through his ministry,
has already been told. He took a particular interest in
that girl ever afterwards. Her behaviour in cleaving to
the Lord's people, in spite of the bitter contempt of her
relations, gave him the greatest satisfaction. And as Mrs.
Parry now tended to frown upon the revival, and to fall
away completely, his affection for Miss Williams began
at times to take a definite shape in his mind. He confesses his fears that something more than a care for her
spiritual welfare played a fundamental part in his interest in her; and as he did with everything else, he laid
this matter open before the Lord. If it had been ordained
that he was to have a wife, he desired that his thoughts
should be led to her. And as he did not receive any
guidance pointing unmistakably to Miss Williams, he
never uttered a syllable to her along those lines for another four years. But at the end of August he wrote to
her and to Mrs. Parry on the same day, urging both of
them that with purpose of heart they should cleave to the
Lord. He tells them that his continual busyness had
caused him to give up all correspondence with many dear
and precious friends; and after these letters, together
with another to his brother Thomas, who was then living
in Paris, we do not possess a single copy of any letter of
his for many months. Thus, one of the sources of the
history of the revival is closed to us for some time yet,
and we have to depend entirely on the diaries.

By now the meetings for psalm-singing had come to an end, and it seemed by every token that this would put a stop to Harris's labours. But somewhat unexpectedly the door was opened, and wider than ever for him, by means of Griffith Jones's Welsh schools. We do not know whether or not he had any part in the decision to found them; but during this autumn he acted as a sort of superintendent over them, and doubtless his labour of love on their behalf was very advantageous to them at their commencement. Mr. Jones's frail health prohibited him from superintending the work in person; and the superintendency could fall into unsuitable hands, as in fact happened later on in North Wales. And yet in spite of the care and anxiety connected with it, Harris was happy in the work because it gave him a splendid opportunity to carry on with his own special work. It was possible for the exhorter to plough with the superintendent's heifer in many ways! His official journeys gave him the opportunity to care for his little flock scattered here and there all over the country, and to drop a word on behalf of Christ to someone continually; and the appointing of teachers made it possible for him to place influential men, chosen from among his converts, in many a dark corner. As far as is known, this was the only payment he received for his work, and he expected nothing more.

"With regard to the schools, Lord, do Thou provide teachers for them; I have done my best. . . . God, I trust, has heard my prayers, and has provided a schoolmaster for Llandyfalle. . . . Received a letter concerning a Welsh school. Anxious that I should not appoint any teacher apart from the will of God. I went to Y Gaer, near Crickhowell. On my way out of church my thoughts were troubled, as a ship is tossed by the waves, on hearing that the schoolmaster had to be a Churchman, and must use the Book of Common Prayer. I was so disheartened that

I could not exhort. I retired to lay the matter before God. Lord, I fear to bring John Powell here, lest he should behave rashly and do harm; and lest that should become a snare to him also, if Thou art calling him to the Baptists. And Oh! Lord! I fear not to do so, lest I should be keeping the light away from this dark corner. The next day, at Llanbedr, near Abergavenny, establishing a Welsh school. Seeking God's mind whom to place there. . . . Thou seest the Welsh schools. Oh! bless them. Thou knowest my aim and purpose—to bring them to know Thee. Oh! do Thou work with us, or our labour will be in vain. I am asked to go around the schools, and to leave my own school. I am ready to go or to stay at home. I wait upon Thee. . . . Near Pains-castle . . . in Llywel . . . in Llygad-yw, etc., catechizing the scholars. Near Dôl-y-gaer, perplexed whether I should go on considering John Powell or not. To the chapel. Trying to reconcile them. Whereas the devil failed to destroy the school through persecutions, he now seems likely to do so effectually by inciting the teachers to dis-sensions. It was God, of His goodness, that kept the school alive, when it had almost perished . . . the many demands for money trouble my thoughts. I lean entirely on Thy Providence for supplies; Thou hast never yet for-saken me. They will trample Thine honour under their feet if I am not able to satisfy their demands: because I am Thy servant. Oh! Lord! shall I not find the means to pay? I do not spend anything on vanities—I would spend all to Thy glory. The care of the schools is upon me. Must I be a burden to my mother, and to everybody else?"

Harris would not have been so free to undertake new tasks were it not that he had an assistant to look after the Talgarth school during his absence. He, in turn, repaid his debt to his young friend by giving him special lessons at school and at home. A warm affection developed between them, and the godliness of the one inflamed the devotion of the other more than ever. In September, the two of them, together with five or six others, consecrated themselves in a written covenant to belong to the Lord for ever. Though Davies did not yet take part in the public work, he prepared himself for it by accompanying his spiritual father on some of his more convenient journeys; and especially by his remarkable attentiveness to all the demands of personal religion. Harris thought so highly of him that he regarded himself as unworthy to be in his company; and at times he was almost jealous of his friend's devotional spirit. "Thank God for giving me so faithful and diligent a companion. Help us to be ready to go throughout the world on Thy behalf. . . . I see Howell to be far better than I am. Today, I could not refrain from eating: my appetite conquered me completely. But Howell fasts and denies himself wonderfully, getting up early to read and to meditate on the Bible, etc. Oh! shall he show more love to Thee than I, who have sinned more against Thee, and received more goodness from Thee? . . . I embraced Howell, and he me, in one another's arms, both of us determined to consecrate ourselves afresh tonight. I prayed for him as usual, and I saw all my former desires for a friend being answered in him. . . . I was much moved by being given to understand that Howell Davies must leave. I went to my bed, and there I wept bitter tears. I found my soul knit to his, as David's was to Jonathan's. I prayed in utter submission to God's will. Oh! Lord! if it is Thy glory which takes him away, I am content. It is Thou who didst give him, and Thou canst take him away." In mid-December, the school broke up, and Harris set out on a three-weeks' journey to visit the societies and schools. When he returned, he found that the authorities had decided to take the school from him. Howell Davies stayed with him for a little while longer; and then, as we have already seen, he went, on Harris's advice, to Llanddowror school.

During the closing months of the year 1737, Harris visited the counties of Carmarthen and Radnor several times; and twice went over to Llangeitho. He also visited some parts of the counties of Monmouth and Hereford, besides caring continually for his own county. Greater crowds gathered to listen to him now. He states that the congregation at Brooks, near Abergavenny, was nearly five hundred; at Merthyr Cynog, although the vicar was a violent persecutor, about four hundred; and in many places round about Builth about five hundred. In Llangeitho the crowd numbered over fifteen hundred; in the Llandovery districts, about a thousand; and in the town itself two thousands souls. He spoke in Welsh or in English, as the circumstances demanded; and oftentimes on the English border he addressed the people in both languages during the same service. It seems that English and Welsh were in use around Trevecka; and his familiarity with both proved to be of great advantage to him in his work.

There were still days when he felt despondent, because of backslidings and oppositions; but now, on the whole, a more confident note is found in his writings. "How often was I in sore straits! In danger of being arrested, yet going on, with my eyes fixed on Jesus Christ! How wonderfully, beyond all expectation, have enemies been softened: Mr. Lloyd, who once threatened to imprison me, has become a friend; and similarly, Sir Humphrey Howarth, and P——n of Glasbury, who were once my greatest enemies but are now milder. From this I learn never to give up. David was strengthened by previous deliverances to face Goliath. . . . The whole country has

been awakened throughout. When I feared I had nothing to say, I spoke best; thus it is God who speaks. The
eyes of my understanding are opened now more than
ever; I can draw five or six, or even seven headings out
of every verse; but I grieve because I cannot remember
them to meditate upon them when I am alone. I find
that the same words and the same reasonings are quite
dead when I lack the authority. . . . On Sunday I went
towards Kilwich. In Llan-gors, I saw them playing, and
I was made the means of stopping them. Towards Wernyberllan. On the way I saw a mill grinding corn, and God
checked them, through me. I was moved at the sight of
ignorance, like a flood, overwhelming everything. . . . Today God enabled me to speak for about nine hours, in
four places. More zeal than ever before, and great success, I hope. If Thou from heaven art sealing my commission, then I am as certain as my head is on my body
that I will never turn back."

As his mind was enlightened with regard to the plan
of salvation, he became more evangelical in spirit, subject
matter, and method. "To Merthyr [Cynog] Church.
Text, John vi. 44. Heard the Doctrine of Free Grace
being pressed home warmly, clearly, and powerfully. Saw
that I had been under a cloud until this hour. I cried
out, 'Oh! Lord! let me hear this wholesome doctrine in
every pulpit.' Never before had I been so stripped of
self. How thankful we should be for a good ministry!
Then, Cwmgwilym. Exhorted against self, and to depend
wholly on Christ. (I had exhorted like this before, but
I had not seen the thing clearly till today. I was not able
to magnify free grace confidently until today.) . . . To
Llowes. More zeal than ever before, with the most moving utterances. . . . On the way home from Wernyberllan.
Fears that God was not in our midst tonight. The sins
of the country lay heavily upon me, and I was dissolved

in tears of sheer pity for nearly two miles. Great affection for God's people: ready to be with them in the mud, or under a hedge, or in a pigsty, rather than be in the palaces of the ungodly. . . . I see that the cords of love are strongest. Those who are drawn to Christ by love are the safest. At first, my preaching consisted entirely of threatenings; and very few were soundly rooted as a result. . . . At Blaen-crai. I spoke for four hours. More order now. A little cowardly because it was vesper time, and because of continual disturbance; but my heart seethed with love and pity for them. I was never so enabled to press the matter home. Very winsome. Very disturbing—especially in the illustration about the worm breeding in a dead man. Great power in showing the gnawings of conscience."

"To a church near Brooks. Sad at seeing such a cold service to God, and such neglect of the people. None of them understood what was said. Then to Llanwenarth Church. Felt compassion for the poor blind people. Then to Dôl-y-gaer. Spoke for three hours. I could not contain myself. It was as if I saw Heaven itself—experiencing it in my soul. Then to Llwynau, in Cwm-du, by eleven at night. Special enabling there, on the journey of the Israelites from Egypt to Canaan. Very tender now, very encouraging. To bed at five in the morning. Arose at eight, and went towards home. I was nearly swept away by the wind on the mountain. In the school my understanding was opened to explain the nature of grace, till five o'clock. Then to Maestorglwyd. . . . At Llywel I began as usual by declaring my love for them; but I fainted so that I was almost like a dead man, and only just managed to finish. To bed there, but I got up at seven in the morning, and went home and to school without breakfast. Oh! strengthen me in body and mind to bring much glory to Thee. In the afternoon I went to

Geuffordd. I was given strength there to be very serious indeed. All on Christ now. . . . To Llywel. Very great help there for three hours. Unusual strength of body and voice; very effectual: thinking it was impossible for them not to be converted. Then private conversations for three hours concerning Election and Reprobation, taking a middle course and avoiding contentions. I controlled them all as I pleased, with great authority. I have now received a remarkable gift for prayer."

It was in this way, then, that Harris spent the closing months of the year 1737: sometimes bemoaning the hardness of the people, as in Llan-arth and the neighbouring districts in Monmouthshire, where great and small so gave themselves to all excesses, that they were too darkened and stupid to give ear to any serious matter; but more often giving praise and wondering at the good effects of his labours. His heart was filled with rejoicing as he beheld the humility and the love of the converts, from Pains-castle, in Radnorshire, down to the lower parts of Brecon-shire. And there were other parts of the country, from beyond the Irfon to beyond the Usk, and across to Llandovery, which had been awakened through them. He still came to the people without any preparation; his head throbbing with pain, his voice hoarse; and he would pour out that which was given him at the time. It is true, that he now divided his matter under headings: the five aspects of man's miserable estate by nature, Christ's six ways of drawing men unto Himself, grace like fire, so many ways, etc., but he did not allow himself to be fettered by headings or anything else. Sometimes the five or six headings would grow into fifteen or twenty; and sometimes they would be completely forgotten. He was particularly direct and personal in dealing with his hearers at this time. If the crowd was too big, he would appeal to them, questioning them one by one, so that one could not hide behind another. Rarely now did he finish without leading them to the sweet comforts of the Gospel.

In the societies, he would select a verse, or a portion of Scripture, to be learnt by each member; with a simple question arising out of it, in order to stimulate them to think. He himself took his verse and his question like the rest. We have seen a copy of the tasks allotted in one society: Watkin Hill to learn the Beatitudes, and to prove the necessity of poverty of spirit, and to show its characteristics; Howell Harris to learn the first Psalm and to show what is meant by sitting in the seat of the scornful, what the wages of following in the way of sinners, and the blessedness of those who do not walk in that way; and Rachel Morgan to learn the verses about the tongue in the Epistle of James, etc. Also, in so far as he was able, he would distribute good books among them. He found in himself a certain reprehensible covetousness for books, with a tendency to look upon them and to be proud of them as his own possession. As a result, in September, he gave all his books to the Lord, to be used to His glory. He made a complete list of them, and wrote at the bottom of it, "God's property." From that time, when he read anything, he regarded the book in his hand as but a loan. He gave away some of them at once to his followers, others he sold in order to meet the expenses of the work; and the rest he kept as a kind of circulating library for the societies. We see that his labours were great in many directions. He thought it would be "a shameful thing that the miser should be more industrious in making money, the wanton in the pursuit of pleasure, or the proud in seeking glory" than he himself was for the glory of his Saviour, and the good of his fellow-men. "Oh," he cried, "that I might do something that would continue to grow after I am gone."

He now became fonder of the Bible, especially of the

Gospel of John. He was much grieved because of his ignorance of its contents, and at one time he determined to write it all down in order to remember it. He vowed again to read a chapter every mid-day on his knees, wherever he might be. One day, he found himself, absentmindedly, eating an apple while reading the Bible; and his spirit was grieved at the thought of the lack of respect he thus showed towards the Word of God. Sometimes in the intensity of his feelings he would press his Bible to his breast, kissing certain passages in the Gospel of John, such as chapter vii. 38. We gather that he did most of his reading while travelling about the country. He was too mercurial by nature to sit down quietly to any task; and if he attempted to do so, sleep would overcome him; and as he was constantly robbing his constitution of the rest necessary to it, he had to pay the price in this way. As soon as he sat down to read, or to listen to a sermon, a real struggle began. Though Griffith Jones, or Daniel Rowland might be in the pulpit, Harris would fall asleep in spite of himself, were it not for his pen. At Llanddowror, at this time, he was so beset by sleep that he used to pinch his flesh till the blood ran, in order to keep himself awake. He retaliated against the flesh by writing, and writing, and writing almost incessantly. One could easily gather the essence of scores of sermons of the old revivalists from his writings. Hundreds of times he was writing nearly the whole night through, when he ought on all accounts to have been in his bed. This is how the mass of MSS. at Trevecka accumulated. It is not surprising that some have found inconsistencies in them. When the circumstances in which they were written are considered, the wonder is that they are as consistent, reliable and appropriate as they are found to be.

But whatever the extent of his reading, he prayed more and more. He did not greatly enjoy public prayer, but in the secret place with his God he was in his element. That was his home—his chiefest pleasure. In Carmarthen at this time, when all the town went out to see the arrival of His Majesty's Judges, Harris stole away to the secret place to pray. At Llangadog, on his way home, he did the same thing instead of joining his companions at dinner. He would retire to the fields—or anywhere—to pray, if he had a moment's leisure. It was in this way that he received all his power and all his comfort. He felt that no one understood him but God. He was so constant in prayer that he was beguiled by the Tempter on many occasions to place too much reliance upon it; and the result was dull and lifeless services. On his knees before the service he would experience glorious feelings; he would then approach the work depending secretly on the prayer and the feeling rather than on Christ; and the meeting would be wholly unsuccessful. At other times he would have a most powerful service, when feeling broken hearted because he had had to set to work without the usual preparation. Through these things he learnt that "prayers, tears and vows are as naught" to depend upon; but he never learnt not to pray. He prayed for all: for himself, for his peevish mother, who almost cursed him when he was on his knees, for his indifferent brothers, for the ungodly world, and for all classes of religious people. This very autumn we find him praying on behalf of the Oxford Methodists—and that is the first reference we find in his writings to the English revivalists.

The more he found a spirit of revival within the Established Church, the more tenaciously did he cling to her. Yet he did not want to be estranged from the Nonconformists either. Some kind of meeting was held by the Nonconformist preachers at Talgarth in September; and he felt a real sense of loss because he did not dare do more than pay them a surreptitious visit. "I have been with the Preachers, and was encouraged. Then to the school. Oh! God! Thou seest how things are! I dare not join with Thy servants today in person to praise Thee, but Lord, my soul is in their midst. I see Presbyterians who have Thy Spirit, and shall I not love them? I see Baptists too, and Quakers of the same type; and are there none in this broken church? Thou seest that her doctrine seems to me to be wholesome, and that it is pity for the people which keeps me within her. Great sorrow because I do not hear Christ being preached, only duties. Either let the Nonconformists come, or else raise up lights among us. I see the Gospel of Christ almost departed from our pulpit. Determined not to hinder any from going to listen to the Nonconformists."

But in spite of his attachment to her, the Church would have none of him except on condition that he be content to be the same as everybody else. In the autumn he received a letter from Mr. Lloyd, definitely commanding him to give up his work. But that, by now, was out of the question. He still wished to be regarded as a candidate for holy orders: and he resolutely states that if he failed to obtain ordination, there would be nothing left to him but to *leave the country*. Hard though that would be, it was easier now to do that than to leave the work. When the school closed for the holidays, the authorities decided that Harris should not re-open it unless he promised to give up everything else. They thought that they could crush and silence him by depriving him of his daily bread, but they only succeeded in setting him free. Behold him then, at the end of 1737, nearly twenty-four years old, going forth from Talgarth, to every practical purpose "a man without any commission under heaven" except to proclaim to his fellow-countrymen the unsearchable riches of Christ.

DEVOTION TO THE WORK
(January-February 1738)

THE new year dawned upon Harris at Llanddowror. On the morrow, in the afternoon, he commenced his journey homewards—here are the details of the itinerary.

January 2. To Meidrim about four c'clock: spoke till about nine: conversed until eleven.

January 3. Spoke for about four hours. Similiarly at Llan-llwch. Powerful services.

January 4. Expounded to the scholars. Then to Llanybydder. There, like Lot in Sodom, vexing his soul in the midst of drunkards and cursers.

January 5. To Cellan, fearful on hearing of the great knowledge of the hearers. Spoke with unusual power for four hours. To Cwmclun-gwyn, near Caeo. Great success there. An open door today.

January 6. To Caeo, weary and in pain. Spoke in the open air to five or six hundred people. No authority. Cil-y-cwm: great authority. Llwynyberllan: unexpected power. To bed after three in the morning.

January 7. To Ystrad-ffin chapel. There until three o'clock, out in the rain, spoke in a melting and rousing manner. To Llanwrtyd, through a real storm of wind and rain. Dripping wet: but wholly indifferent to his condition—singing Psalms the whole way. Very great authority there.

January 8. Spoke until ten o'clock with power as last night. Then to the church. The Parson read with such lack of understanding that he was afraid that by staying there, he would be guilty of the sin of mocking the Almighty. Afternoon, in Cefnllysgwyn. Evening, at Builth, with wisdom and power.

January 9. Going homeward, ill and lifeless. Heard, at Talgarth, that he had lost the school. No trace of worry. Proving the fulfilment of the promises of Psalm xxxii. 6, 7. "I am off all worldly helps: and rest easy on Thee."

But though he spoke in this way, an occasional wave of anxiety broke over him. With no money in hand, and none in prospect; the necessities of life demanding satisfaction; a debt to his mother calling for payment; it is surprising that he could muster enough courage to hold on to his work. It seems that he still kept some sort of school in his home at Trevecka; Howell Davies and others still held loyally to him; and he himself found it very difficult to be fair to them without refusing the calls now pouring in upon him from all directions. We imagine that he aimed at preparing them to be teachers in the Welsh schools; or perhaps to help him in his public work. But whatever might have to suffer, the fields white unto the great harvest must not be neglected. Before the end of the week he took a short journey in the direction of Herefordshire. He spoke at Maestorglwyd, Cornelmelyn, and in another place four miles south of Hay, Park, Olchon —to eight hundred people for over six hours, in Welsh and English. Llanigon—from midnight till cock-crow. Cusop—in Welsh and English, and Maes-gwyn—with the boldness of a lion on Jeremiah xlviii. 10. When he reached home, he found a messenger awaiting him to summon him to appear once more before the governors of Talgarth school. He prayed earnestly before going. On the way he took a Bible from his pocket and asked God to show him His will there and then. The Book opened at Rev. iii. 8-11, and all anxiety vanished in

a moment. He spoke before the gentlemen as one having authority, realising that he was there to defend
the cause of the Most High. He went out of the
council joyfully, praying that God would bless his
words to bring the persecuting Parson to the light and
to make him an instrument for the enlightenment of
others.

On Thursday, 19 January, he set out on a journey, or
rather, a series of other journeys. He paid a visit to the
lower parts of the county and the districts around Abergavenny. He paid brief visits to his scholars at Trevecka
in the afternoon of the Monday and of the Tuesday. On
Wednesday he was at Sirhywi, near Nant-y-glo [in Mon-
mouthshire]. That night, at Llygad-yw, he had one of
the most remarkable experiences of his life. Although
his body was weak and aching, and though he could eat
nothing, the realities of the spiritual world appeared so
naked and open to his mind throughout the time that his
weak body was clothed with unparalleled power, so that
his very appearance dispelled all opposition. He was
home for a few hours on Thursday afternoon; and that
night he was at Pentre Iago, more or less ineffectively.
He passed through the border of Radnorshire and
reached Builth by Saturday night. On Sunday he was at
Llanwrtyd till after midnight; and it was at four o'clock
in the morning at Llwynyberllan, near Llandovery, that
he found himself a bed. Next day he spoke without much
enjoyment to about a thousand people near Cil-y-cwm
church. After discussion with the schoolmasters he
went on to fulfil his engagements: Llwyncynyris, Cwm-
y-dŵr by Llanwrda, and Glangwydderig—where he
had about two thousand to hear him, and a delightful
service. He was thankful these days for the favourable weather, which allowed him to preach in the open
air.   He made his way homewards through Blaen-

clydach, Llywel, Cray, Brychgoed, Bolgoed (where he finally heard that he had lost the school), Maesybeddau, Llaneglwys, Llandyfalle, reaching Trevecka on Monday, 6 February.

But for Howell Davies, he could expect little comfort now at home. But he was pleasantly surprised. Letters from Bristol awaited him, and in them the story of the activities of the English revivalist, George Whitefield. He was overwhelmed by emotion as he read them, and glorifying God for Mr. Whitefield, he declared himself anew to his Saviour. "Oh! Jesus Christ—squeezing Him spiritually in my arms—I dedicate myself to Thee." He treasured every word he read of Whitefield after this, until the two met at Cardiff about thirteen months later. Two days later he went to Gwenddwr to hear Mr. Rowland, and the service proved a wonderful blessing to him. Rowland preached from Proverbs viii. 31, exalting the love of Christ in such an effective manner that one, at least, of his hearers was taken completely captive by this most powerful love. Harris saw depths of love in the word and the promises that he had never imagined before. He saw Christ pleading on his behalf in Heaven, and he felt that he was beginning to know something of the love which passeth knowledge. "Today was an extraordinary day to my soul." As we have mentioned in a previous chapter, Harris often said afterwards that it was on that day—8 February 1738—in Gwenddwr church, that he was led to a true knowledge of Christ. He had thought highly of Rowland before. He had heard that he was such a diligent student that he had lost his hair; and when he experienced in his own proud heart, as he says, an inclination to compare himself with him, he would castigate himself without mercy for doing so. But from this day forward the curate of Llangeitho occupied the highest place in Harris's estimation and affection; and it is doubtful whether anyone more worthy of honour than he ever made an appearance or threatened to make him take a lower place.

When he returned home he received a letter from Griffith Jones, and we gather that its contents were not so pleasing to him. It is probable that Mr. Jones was trying to force him back to the school again, or else trying to persuade him to lie low until he was given church orders.[1] But it was too late. Come what might, the work must be carried forward. On Friday, he spoke at Pentre Tregoed, in Welsh and English, most pleasantly. On Saturday, at Trecradoc and other places, full of love. On Sunday he was in Dorston church, Herefordshire; and that night he had a most remarkable English service at Broadmeadow. On Monday he crossed the borders of Radnorshire to Aberedw, where he preached mainly in English and that so powerfully that he had to stay with the people until broad daylight. On the morrow he was at Skreen, Gwenddwr and Llangoed, and got to bed at Llannerch Goedlan at three o'clock in the morning. But he was constrained in his spirit to retire in secret prayer, and he rose without delay to give yet another hour to this task. He spent some time with his scholars mid-week; but on Friday night he was at Dôl-y-gaer, where—from the story of the prophet Elijah and the widow of Zarephath—his faith with regard to his daily bread was strengthened. On the morrow, after a service in the chapel, where he heard John Powell giving his experience, he went to Llanwenarth to address the "critical Baptists," and by depending wholly on Christ he received effective aid. On Sunday, Abergavenny and Llangattock

[1] Bennett never saw this letter, but of late years it has been discovered. It is dated Feb. 5, 1737/8. Griffith Jones discusses matters dealing with the Welsh schools; he does not mention Harris's old school at Talgarth at all, neither does he refer to ordination.—G. M. R.

[near Usk];[1] and Monday, Dôl-y-gaer, Capel-y-ffin, Maestorglwyd and Felindre. He called at Trevecka for some hours on Tuesday morning, and in the afternoon he set out for Carmarthenshire. His body was so wasted that he could hardly move, but his energy was strangely revived at Llandeilo'r-fân next morning while reading of the revival in New England. He went on through Llanddeusant, Llangadog and Llanwrda fairly well, yet without much authority. But on Friday, at Talyllychau the authority returned, and the result was altogether indescribable—the hoarse voice cleared and became terribly powerful, streams of words and scriptural texts poured into the mind of the preacher, and through him to the hearers; and a power to convict people and lead them to Christ given to him, such as he had never experienced before. That night, at Pen-y-banc in the parish of Llanfynydd, we must leave him, because the diary ends here, and a gap of over four months occurs in the records. We only know that he proceeded on his journey to Llangeitho and the surrounding districts, where he spent the first days of March.

[1] Griffith Jones, in a post-script to the above letter, writes as follows: "If you send a list of your Welsh schools to cousin (?) Dd. Jones, curate of Llangattock Juxta Usk, perhaps he may find time to see some of them & hear them examined."—G. M. R.

NEW FIELDS AND WORKERS
(March-June 1738)

IT is regrettable that we have to deal with such an interesting period in the history of the revival without the guidance of the diary or the letters. We have to gather our scanty material here and there from stray references to this period in Harris's reminiscences during later years.

There had been but little intercourse between Harris and the Presbyterians, or the Independents, before this time. The first of them to take any interest in the revival movement, as far as we know, was Mr. Rees Davies, minister of the Independent church at Abergavenny. Mr. Davies was a kinsman of Mr. Evan Davies, minister of the same denomination at Haverfordwest in Pembrokeshire, one of the best men of his age. They appear to have kept up a more or less constant correspondence with each other, and it would be quite natural for Rees Davies to inform his kinsman of the religious stirrings in the eastern counties. We have evidence also that Griffith Jones of Llanddowror thought highly of the Catholic spirit of the minister from Haverfordwest; and that they corresponded occasionally. All these things considered, it is probable that Evan Davies knew a great deal about the revival in its early stages; and we gather that it was he who invited Harris to Pembrokeshire in the summer of 1737. We know that Harris considered Mr. Evan Davies as one of his best friends for years; and we believe it is he, of all the Independent ministers, who has the honour of being the first to seek to enlarge the sphere of the revival's influence. But in the spring of 1738 the time had come for others to follow his example.

Some time in March, Harris went on a journey to Herefordshire, and somewhere there he met Mr. Edmund Jones, an assistant minister at a branch of the Independent church at Pen-maen, Monmouthshire. Perhaps he had never hitherto met anyone possessed of a spirit so like his own in some respects. We gather that Mr. Jones was neither learned nor eloquent; but he was full of a desire to do good wherever he might be. He had been preaching for ten years before he was ordained to the ministry; and it appears that he acted to some extent as a free-lance in the service of his Master, visiting churches which happened to be in need of pastoral care in various parts of the country. When he now heard, for the first time, the powerful ministry of Howell Harris, he felt like one who had found great spoil; and nothing would satisfy him but that his neighbours in Monmouthshire should enjoy the same privilege. It appears that Gwent and Glamorgan—both gentry and common people —gave themselves up more completely to all forms of dissipation than any other part of Wales. The Parson of Defynnog wrote to Harris saying that there was more desecration of the Sabbath in the Diocese of Llandaff than in any other place known to him. It was of the inhabitants of the same district that John Wesley wrote that they were "as utterly ignorant as any Creek or Cherokee Indians" in America. Better things might have been expected. Leaving out of account the ample provision made by the Established Church for the spiritual needs of the population, this was the cradle of Welsh Nonconformity, this was the home of its princes, Edmund Jones and Miles Harry, and this was the place most likely to have experienced the benefits of the alleged revival of 1730. But, in spite of all this, a darkness which could be felt shrouded these regions still; and the Methodist Fathers scarcely received a worse reception anywhere than they did in Monmouthshire. It is too unsatisfactory an explanation to attribute this to Howell Harris's rashness and indiscretion; because he was exactly the same man here as he was in other places. Besides this, John Wesley had a very unfriendly reception in Monmouthshire, and he could scarcely be charged with indiscretion. This shows that Nonconformity had not yet become a great power for good, even in its own habitat. Nearly all their best men stood on the defensive, not having developed the gift—nor the courage—to carry the war boldly into the enemy's territory. Of them all, there is no doubt that Edmund Jones was the most ready in spirit to say, "Let us go in and possess the land"; but even he did not have the power to draw the crowds after him, and to persuade them to forsake ungodliness. Like Simeon of old, he was a righteous and a very godly man, waiting earnestly for better times; or, according to Mr. Whitefield's words, he was a Zacharias, and his wife an Elisabeth. But no one ever thought of saying that he was like their son—able to stir an entire nation out of their spiritual apathy. When Edmund Jones heard the new prophet in Herefordshire, he rejoiced with exceeding joy, and did not rest till he got him to proclaim his message in the districts of Ponty-pool and Mynyddislwyn. This took place, it seems, in April; and it is said that the visit proved a great blessing to many people, but we have no particulars to add to what we already know of it. We can only mention that it was in the spring of 1739—not at this time, as stated by our historians—that Mr. Perrot, the incumbent of Mynyddislwyn, wrote to Harris demanding that he keep away from his parishes.

It is certain that the meeting between Harris and Edmund Jones turned out to the great advantage of the revival. Although the latter was older in years, higher in office, and a rigid Nonconformist, he greatly humbled himself to be a kind of armour-bearer to the young layman of the Established Church. He did his best to arrange itineraries for him: to bring him to the notice of the most awakened ministers in Wales and England, in order to encourage him; and to provide for his bodily needs. Harris at this time did not possess a penny, nor did he have the opportunity of earning anything towards his livelihood. Mrs. Parry of Tal-y-llyn, who had been so kind to him in the past, was declining rapidly in health; and perhaps Mr. Gwynne of Garth had not yet been aroused to a sense of duty towards his father in the Gospel. However that may be, it seems that it was Edmund Jones, either by giving sacrificially out of his own deep poverty, or by being a channel to convey the goodwill of the friends of religion in England, who was instrumental in keeping Harris from want during the coming months. Many times Harris's heart leapt for joy at receiving a few shillings from his Great Master through the hands of his fellow-servant from Monmouthshire. He was of considerable service to him in another way too. As is often the case with men of strong passions, Harris fell at times into fits of deep dejection; and there was no one like Edmund Jones for raising him out of the dungeon. Indeed, he says more than once that the praises and kindness of Edmund Jones would have spoilt him had not the Lord sent Griffith Jones of Llanddowror and James Roberts of Ross to keep him down.

It seems that the displeasure of his brethren and of the majority of the fellowship at Pen-maen, was the only reward that Mr. Jones received for his Christian behaviour. The following year, a man eight to ten years younger than himself in age, as man, church member and preacher, was chosen as assistant minister to the church

and all its branches. This man was well known all his
life as the opposer of all things pertaining to Methodism;[1]
and we gather that he and the old minister made things
so uncomfortable for Edmund Jones that the latter felt
impelled to sever his connection entirely with Pen-maen,
and to found a new cause near the town of Pont-y-pool.
He was of great help in connection with the revival for
a time. He was gifted with the ability of caring for the
young converts; and there was scarcely a limit to his in-
dustry and faithfulness in his own particular sphere. We
believe that Harris consulted him more than any other
man during the next two years. After this time differences of opinion caused a certain amount of estrangement
between them, but no sign of anything approaching enmity; and in the evening of their days, their old friendship was re-kindled.

Among Harris's hearers in Monmouthshire was Mr.
David Williams of Pwll-y-pant, the minister of the Independent churches of Watford and Cardiff, who urged
him earnestly to visit parts of Glamorgan. Around Whit-
suntide he was there for two days, and according to Mr.
Williams's testimony his labour was crowned with unusual success. "The churches and the meetings are
crowded," writes Mr. Williams; "Sabbath-breaking is declining, it is looked upon as a very detestable thing; dancing has been much hindered; profane swearing and cock-
fighting are protested against." On some of these journeys
he came into contact with other Glamorgan ministers—
Mr. Henry Davies, Blaen-gwrach; Mr. Joseph Simmons,
Neath; and Mr. James Davies of Merthyr Tydfil—who,

---

[1] Bennett refers here to Philip David, who—in 1739—was
ordained as assistant minister to David Williams, the senior
minister of Pen-maen. His unpublished diaries reflect his strong
prejudice against the Methodist "way" of preaching which was
gaining ground in those days amongst the Welsh Nonconformists.—G. M. R.

as Mr. Williams had done, urged him earnestly to visit their districts too. But, in trying to respond to these increasing invitations, he expended so much of his energy, that his constitution could not stand the strain any longer. He broke down completely for a few weeks about the beginning of this summer, and the expectations of thousands of people who had come to see and to hear him were disappointed. But he was given no peace even on his sick bed. The ministers wrote to him again and again, beseeching him to hasten into their midst and assuring him that the ardour of the people to hear him was such that neither the harvest nor anything else would be allowed to prevent them from coming to meet him. And when he could not go down to meet them because of his weakness, about twenty people from Glamorgan came all the way to Trevecka to see how he was; and opening their treasures, they offered presents to the Lord's servant and stayed with him for a few days listening to his teaching, to the great profit of their hungry and thirsty souls.

His diary from the middle of June to the beginning of July is still extant. He spent most of this time at home. A private room was now placed at his disposal—perhaps by his aunt—and he felt especially grateful for such a favour. Physically he was very weak, his chest painful, and so wasted in appearance that when he saw his face in a glass one day, he believed that the hour of his dissolution was at hand. He prayed much for the societies, and he tried to visit those nearest to him. It seems that he wrote a set of Rules or Regulations for them at this time, but no copy of this has been seen. He often mentions the wonderful kindness shown him by the family of Dôl-y-gaer, and when he heard of Mrs. Rumsey's illness he determined to visit her, spending a Sunday at Cwm Iau on the way. Although he could not exhort as he used to, his pale and austere appearance, together with his

F

earnestness, nevertheless helped to make his brief addresses very powerful. While returning home, he passed by the spot on the mountain where he had experienced the brightness of God's face shining upon his soul in such a remarkable manner sometime previously, when he received the gift of "spiritualising" things, and his spirit was made tender at the thought that God was still the same. The journey had been too much for him; his strength was failing almost to the point of exhaustion; and three weary miles lay between him and home. But he looked with faith to God to restore his feeble body, and lo, behold him walking home as sprightly, "as in the best days ever."

He was at home during the whole of the following week, in his room for the most part, praying for the labourers who had been carrying on the work while he had been confined—Edmund Jones, Enoch Francis,[1] and Daniel Rowland. He had heard, with joy, of the divine unction which had attended the latter's ministry. He was comforted, too, by hearing of the triumphant death of Jack of Cwm-hwnt, a servant lad in a nearby farm, remembering his devoted life—how on his knees he had struggled to learn to read, how he rose from his bed to pray, how he made it a condition of employment that he could have time off to hear the Word, and how he repaid fourfold the people who had suffered any loss through him. He was not hindered by persecutions or temptations; but, with an assured testimony of his portion in Christ, he faced death singing Psalms and exhorting all to take the Kingdom of Heaven by force. It did Harris good to know of this seal upon his ministry. It strengthened his heart for the receiving of very different news—

[1] A Baptist minister, who lived at Penygelli, near Newcastle Emlyn; he died in 1740 after a very successful ministry. He was an ardent Calvinist and an earnest preacher.—G. M. R.

of societies north of Brecon falling away, of seekers becoming restless, and of good men prophesying that his
practice of going about the country would bring misfor-
tunes, if not shame, on religion. This short spell of sickness and comparative idleness gave the enemy the opportunity to attack him from many directions, and it is
painful to read his bitter reproaches against himself. He
was worse than anyone, baser than all men, unfit to come
within miles of the congregation of the saints; and his
present illness was an indication from the Lord that his
service was unacceptable.

In order to seek deliverance from the body of this
death, he turned to the place where he found it many
times, before and after, that is at the Lord's Table. He
made his way to Merthyr Cynog for the Sunday, praying
that God would keep the vicar at home, so that the curate
might have the place to himself. On the way there he
came across *The Sincere Convert*, the book that proved
such a blessing to him afterwards. The converts were
already tending to gravitate to Merthyr on Sundays; and
Harris feared that the presence of so many strangers
would arouse the ire of the vicar against Thomas Lewis,
the curate, whose teaching was so acceptable to the
people. From there he went on to Bolgoed, right among
those who were tending to draw back, where he chanced
to meet Howell Davies. We do not know where Davies
now spent his time. It seems almost certain that there
was some connection between him and the family, or district, of Bolgoed.[1] However that may be, his relation had
taken such a hold on him, that it is fairly certain that he
had not undertaken any secular work. Some time after
this, his diary for July 1738 was found, in which he says

[1] Bennett was right, of course (see footnote, p. 129). William
Williams of Bolgoed was Davies's uncle, and he was probably
staying at Bolgoed during these weeks.—G. M. R.

that at that time he had such an experience of God's love, for a whole week, that he could not bear to hear a single word about the world. He hardly slept at all during the whole of this time, and when he took some food, he seemed to have no sense of taste. He felt as if his soul was in the presence of the cherubim of glory. We gather that it was at that time that Harris advised him to go to Llanddowror.

After reaching home Harris spent several days in his "room" resting and reading *The Sincere Convert*. That book inflamed his zeal for the plan of God's grace more than ever. He drew away, more and more, from Arminianism even in its moderate form, because he feared that this was but sugary bait, as it were, to entice people into swallowing its more extreme forms. He was also able to enjoy a good deal of the company of his old friend, Joseph Saunders, and reviewing the beginnings of the work proved to be most refreshing to both of them. He also received a most encouraging letter from Mr. Edmund Jones, when he was on the verge of giving up the work altogether because of his weakness. He set out with the intention of being at Cwm Iau on the coming Sunday. On the Saturday he spoke for over seven hours, in Welsh and English, in various places in Herefordshire[1] till he found himself practically exhausted; and he failed to arrive at Cwm Iau next day in time for the service. He no longer loved John Powell as he had once done, but he could not refrain from offering long and earnest prayers on his behalf. On Monday, although weak in body, he went to Llanbedr wake[2] to urge the revellers in a most

[1] Welsh was spoken in many districts of Herefordshire, on the Welsh border, in the eighteenth century.—G. M. R.

[2] The yearly wake—*gwylmabsant* in Welsh—was held in great regard in many Welsh parishes in the eighteenth century. It was held, as a rule, to celebrate the local saint's birthday or the day of his death.—G. M. R.

endearing way to turn to Christ. He rested that night with the kind family of Dôl-y-gaer, and on the morrow, at Llygad-yw—as there is another gap in the records—we must leave him, complaining bitterly against his old enemy. "Oh! Lord! if Thou wilt not kill this, it will kill me. 'Tis mixed with all I do: follows me to my private and public duties. Oh! Lord! slay, slay, slay—this villain—my dreadful enemy, self."

NEW FIELDS AND WORKERS
(continued)
(July-August 1738)

WE do not know how Harris spent the month of July; but we have grounds to believe that he was near the borders of Montgomeryshire about that time. Some time before August he paid a visit to Mr. David Lewis of Cwmteuddwr, whose ministry had been a blessing to him. Perhaps it was this time too that he became acquainted with another man from Radnorshire, namely, Mr. Vavasor Griffiths, an Independent minister and Master of the Nonconformist Academy. Mr. Griffiths was truly one of the best men of his age: the best man that Edmund Jones ever knew, and he did not expect to meet his like until he reached the better land. It is difficult to understand why the history of such an excellent man has been so completely lost.[1] There is but a brief note on him in Rees and Thomas's *History of the Welsh Independent Churches,* and even some of that is misleading. His church at Maes-gwyn was not a branch of Maesyronnen; but it belonged to the ministerial circuit of Knighton, as may be seen in Dr. John Evans's lists. Neither did he live in the south of the county, but in the parish of Bugeildy, in its northern extremity. It is possible that he was descended from one of the two Griffiths, who were licensed as Independent preachers in Bugeildy in 1672—and also from the Vavasors who formerly lived on the border of Montgomeryshire, Radnor-

[1] Since Bennett wrote, much information in connection with Vavasor Griffiths has come to light—see Dr. R. T. Jenkins's article in the *Dictionary of Welsh Biography.*—G. M. R.

shire and Shropshire.[1] It appears that he was in comfortable circumstances, and held in high esteem in church circles and in the world at large. Doctrinally, he was regarded as orthodox as any in his denomination; and at the same time wider in his sympathies and warmer in his spirit than perhaps any of them. He was a bosom friend to Harris and to the revival to the end. During the last months of his life, he and his Academy moved to Chancefield, near the town of Talgarth; and often did Harris turn to him for comfort and advice in the midst of all the troubles connected with the work. By then many of the Nonconformists were withholding their co-operation, and the love of Edmund Jones seemed to be growing cold. The bogey was the Arminianism of the two Wesleys, and the fact that Harris kept up his friendship with them, preaching the duty of striving to reach the experience of assurance of salvation, so that it led many of his hearers to doubt whether he were not teaching the sinless perfection of the Wesleys. This, in our judgment, more than any difference of opinion with regard to church polity, caused the estrangement between the Nonconformists and the Methodists. But Harris found in Vavasor Griffiths a tower of defence until his death; and bitter indeed was his sorrow at the early death, in 1741, of "the fairest flower of his denomination." The death of David Lewis and of Vavasor Griffiths within the same year was a great loss to Radnorshire. The mortal remains of the latter lie in the parish churchyard of Bugeildy, but we do not know whether or not there is a tombstone to mark his grave.

[1] According to the late Rev. John Davies, Pandy—no mean authority—a near relation of Vavasor Griffiths—his brother, possibly—lived at Esgair Berfedd in the parish of Llanfair-ar-y-bryn, Carmarthenshire; he came there during the time of persecution in the 17th century. This man, David Griffiths, baptised a son named Vavasor in 1743.—G. M. R.

The Glamorgan ministers continued to plead with Harris to visit them again. He had been to some parts of mid-Glamorgan some time before this; he had preached at Betws [Tir Iarll, not far from Maesteg] and other places, and he had promised to return again. It is in the vicinity of Dôl-y-gaer where we left him at the beginning of July, that we find him at the end of the month on his way to fulfil his promise. By this time his health was sufficiently restored to enable him to preach to great crowds with great power and authority. He went through Monmouthshire from Llanwenarth to Llanbradach; and across Glamorgan from Llanedern to Neath; and then on through Llanelli, reaching Llanddowror on Saturday night, 12 August. Passing through Carmarthen, Llan-ddeusant, and Llywel he returned home by the end of the following week.

An open rebellion against Heaven prevailed through-out Gwent and Glamorgan at that time, which made doubly valuable the faithfulness of the few witnesses found there. Harris met with opposition in various forms during this journey. In a place called St. Lythan's Moun-tain, between Llanishen and St. Nicholas, a clergyman came to threaten him, and a solicitor to upset the meet-ing, causing a great disturbance. A constable was ordered to take the preacher into custody; his friends were mocked and vilified; but the storm soon blew over. He experienced a more savage attack in Llantrisant church on Sunday. A special service was held there in the after-noon, and an able sermon was delivered in his hearing obviously designed for his special benefit. The theme was spiritual pride. It was shown that true humility keeps its possessor out of sight, restraining him from set-ting his mind on things too high for him, and from in-terfering in other people's affairs—that the philosophers of old trembled when they went to teach the public—

that Moses, because of a feeling of inadequacy, tried to evade the work to which he had been called as long as he could—and that our Blessed Saviour did not begin to teach until he was a full thirty years of age. But now, behold mere ignorant striplings were going about the country, taking upon themselves the dread responsibility of being religious teachers. This was a generation clean in its own sight, but which had never been cleansed from its defilement, etc., etc.

Poor Howell Harris! He had felt before that he was a great sinner, but now he felt that the worst thing he had ever done was to go about exhorting. His soul was drowned in misery. He determined that never again would he leave home. Full of humility, he approached the clergyman at the end of the service, submitting to every reproach and indignity. Full of doubts and dread, he went to the crowd, as a man without reproofs on his lips. Full of shame he went to the house; but God took all authority away from him everywhere. It was a very good thing indeed that he met the godly and kind Mr. Henry Davies at Ystradyfodwg [Rhondda] the next day and had the opportunity of conferring with him as to what to do. He proceeded on his way, not very willingly, and on Tuesday afternoon, at Neath Abbey, where three thousand people awaited his coming, the authority was restored to him, and the storm abated. It was a powerful service, and he had much pleasure in the company of Henry Davies, Joseph Simmons, and William Thomas, the vicar of Llanilltud; in addition he received a present of five shillings and sixpence, which made him feel that he must retire on his own to praise God for causing goodness and mercy to follow him in this way continually. On his way toward the west he heard that the press-gang was in Llanelli; but he went on, ready to go to the war if that was God's will.

It is difficult to understand exactly Harris's relationship with Griffith Jones at this time. For some time he had felt a certain reluctance to go to Llanddowror, and he often declared that he could never live at ease with the "strict saints". It seems that the family discipline was fairly strictly and exactly ordered there, especially in Mrs. Bevan's house in Laugharne and that he too was compelled to take part in the learning and the reciting, and the public prayers—things for which he had never had much taste. In addition, every complaint laid against him always arrived there before him, so that it was mainly a sense of duty that drove him there now. For some time now Mr. Jones's attitude towards his work had been one of toleration rather than approval, and we find Harris praying for help to be indifferent to what was said about him, not only by the evil-minded, but also by good men. But after being there he always blessed the Lord for the benefit he had received during his visit. He needed the severity of Llanddowror to salt other people's applause.

During this journey he lost one of his benefactors, but found others to take her place. Mrs. Parry of Tal-y-llyn, his old patroness, was sinking rapidly. He had been anxious about her ever since he left home, and near Bolgoed, on his return journey, he heard the news that she had died. He was quite overcome, and immediately left the company to be alone. "Oh! God! sanctify this to me," he cried. "Keep mine eyes from looking upon a woman; let no creature share Thy place. The thought that she will never pray any more, nor receive advice any more, drove the matter many degrees deeper into my soul than anything else ever did before. I wept so copiously and so bitterly, that I was almost broken. Great searchings of heart as to what has become of her. Is she in the glory? Some ground for hoping from the deep desires that God poured into my soul on her behalf, in Blaenau Gwent, that I shall meet her soul in Heaven." He felt that his levity of spirit had been completely destroyed now, and eternity impressed so solemnly upon his mind that he could never smile again. He could not bear to look at Tal-y-llyn mansion on his way home, as

> "The fairest pearl within it
> Was now silent in the grave."

He was accompanied on this journey by a young man named Jenkin. We meet him first in the Neath district; and we take it that he was the same person known later as Jenkin Morgan of Rhos-y-meirch, Anglesey. The authors of the *History of the Welsh Independent Churches* tend to think that he was a native of the Caerphilly district, and a member of Watford church. On the other hand, John Hughes, in his history of Welsh Methodism, states that he came from Carmarthenshire. I am of the opinion that some part of the Vale of Neath has the honour of being the birthplace of this good man. We know that he was a communicant in one of Henry Davies's churches before he became a member of Llanddowror church on his appointment as schoolmaster; but it is impossible to decide whether he was originally a Nonconformist, or one of Harris's converts who had joined a Nonconformist church for a time, like Thomas Price of Watford. However, the above fact lends some support to Dr. Thomas Rees's statement that Griffith Jones did employ Nonconformists as teachers. Jenkin Morgan soon became known. In February 1739, he went to Montgomeryshire, and from henceforward he laboured mainly in the northern counties of Wales, and we believe that North Wales owes more to him than has been hitherto realised. Is it possible that the Jenkin Morgan of the Vale of Neath who opened his house to receive the ark of the Lord at the beginning of the last century, be of the same family? Perhaps someone with local knowledge will make further research into the matter.[1]

Harris's friendship with the Independents did not cause him to break with the Baptists. When he came home, he received, through William Herbert, a letter from James Roberts, a Baptist minister of Ross in Herefordshire, which was the beginning of an intimate and long-lasting relationship. His home life was still rather troubled. He rejoiced to see in his mother some signs of concern about the state of her soul; and on the other hand he was saddened at the thought of the difficulties. "Oh! that I knew what to do with respect to Evan and John Powell. Lord, if Thou art sending them, bless them; but if Thou art not, restrain them. Let no harmful consequences follow what we are doing. Everything is in Thy hands. . . . Afraid I am doing that which is not right, in view of the fact that the parsons are opposing everywhere— and more especially as they in Llanddowror are doing so—and also because I myself was brought to the same conclusion, at Llantrisant. Then again, I hear the call of the Nonconformists! but I fear they are moved by a party spirit. Oh! Lord! my soul is indeed in agony. Hold Thou me up; I leave everything in Thy hands.

But though his feelings were very changeable, Harris still went on. We have now accompanied him through all the counties of South Wales, except Pembrokeshire; and we now have the pleasure of seeing him turning his face towards the North. Among the churches which had been served by Edmund Jones before his ordination, was

---

[1] Bennett refers to Jenkin Morgan, of Maesmarchog, mentioned by Rees and Thomas, *op. cit.*, ii. 112. Against Bennett's opinion that Jenkin Morgan came from the Vale of Neath we may cite the fact that his name is not found in a list of the members of Cwm-gwrach congregation, made by Henry Davies in 1734. He might have joined later, of course.—G. M. R.

the Nonconformist church of Llanbryn-mair in Mont-gomeryshire. It was a mixed congregation of Indepen-dents and Baptists; and it cannot be said that perfect con-cord always existed between the two parties. Because of this the church had been for some time without a min-ister and it was during this period that Edmund Jones visited them. But the Baptists soon increased in number until they were in a position to invite a brother of their own denomination to take the charge of the church. He, too, was a Monmouthshire man, but it is likely that Edmund Jones could not agree to this, good Christian though he was; because sometime before this he had en-gaged in a prolonged and heated controversy with the Baptists, and displayed too much narrowmindedness to-wards that sect right to the end. The new minister was ordained in April 1733. But uneasiness arose in the church with regard to certain articles in his doctrine, so that he left the following year.[1] This gave Edmund Jones his opportunity. He did not delay long before visiting Llanbryn-mair again, and found the place without a min-ister, and pretty thoroughly swept and garnished. He decided immediately to return to South Wales to fetch —not an evil spirit but a very good one, better indeed than himself—and to bring him back with him, and to settle him in the vacant place, to hold it in possession for Christ and for Independency.

He had no need to go far. As we have already seen, the Independent Academy had been moved that year from Carmarthen to Maes-gwyn, in the north of Radnor-shire. Edmund Jones made his way there. Among the students there was a young man from the Vale of Neath named Lewis Rees, or Rice. It is said that he was of a

---

[1] His name was Benjamin Meredith, of Llanwenarth. After returning home he fell again into theological controversy and he was excommunicated.—G. M. R.

lovable disposition from his boyhood, and although he was but a first-year student in the Academy he had been educated in preparatory schools under Henry Davies, Joseph Simmons, and Rees Price of Bridgend. These three were uncompromisingly orthodox, so that their pupils were not in the same danger of having their spirits vexed by the heretical ideas that troubled many of the students at Carmarthen. Under their care, and that of Mr. Vavasor Griffiths, his present tutor, the young man's powers and character had speedily developed in such a wholesome atmosphere; and as soon as Edmund Jones revealed his purpose in coming, the lot fell upon him at once as the young man most fitted to take charge of a church. Edmund Jones promised to accompany him to Llanbryn-mair, to introduce him to the fellowship there; and about the autumn of 1734 (in our opinion) the two men were on their way. Perhaps the story of that journey is well known to the reader—how the night caught up with them on the hills of Carno, how they lost their way and wandered for a long time in the Fron woods, how joyful communion with Heaven kept their fears in check, and how they arrived at their lodging at Tŷ-mawr almost without knowing it at two o'clock in the morning, and Edmund Jones's remarkable prayer on the occasion. The church was pleased with the young man, and he was invited to settle among them, and time proved the wisdom of the choice. He laboured diligently and usefully in the Montgomeryshire area, and indeed in many of the other counties of North Wales, and his memory will abide as a sweet smelling savour from generation to generation.

In April 1738, at the time of Howell Harris's first visit to the Pont-y-pool district, and the beginning of his association with the Independents, Lewis Rees came down south to be ordained to the full work of the ministry. It seems that the two met somewhere at that time. It would be extremely interesting to know the story of their meeting together, but the diary is missing. We know, however, that Rees pressed Harris for a promise to visit Montgomeryshire until he obtained it. On the back of a letter which Harris received in April we find the following words: "Direct for the Rev. Mr. Lewis Rees at Llanbryn-mair. To be left at the Post Office, Newtown. Turn at Gloucester. From Rhaeadr to Llanidloes, 7 miles, and eight miles to Llanbryn-mair."

But four months passed by before the promise was fulfilled. In spite of hearing that he would be in danger of being "pressed" into the army before he returned, behold him on Saturday, 19 August, setting out on a journey to North Wales for the first time. As he left he was troubled to find in himself a spirit of pride—pride at seeing his mother and himself so well-dressed, and shame because their house was so mean. "Wilt Thou hold Thy treasure-store of graces before me, for the hand of faith to draw out of it? Lord, what I desire is humility, and the power to do all things to Thy glory. Behold here an abundance of graces, and this is what I crave as my portion." He partook of the Sacrament at Merthyr Cynog on Sunday, and lodged near Builth that night. We do not know how he spent the hours of day or night on Monday, as some pages of the records are missing. He called on Mr. Lewis at Cwmteuddwr, and on Tuesday afternoon, at about three o'clock, he arrived at the town of Llanidloes, his first stopping place in North Wales.

EPILOGUE
(By the Translator)

THE foregoing chapters give an account of Howell Harris's life and labours up to August 1738. The story of his conversion, his preaching, and the founding of the first societies, is, in fact—as the Welsh title of Richard Bennett's book suggests—the story of the beginning of the Methodist Revival in Wales. It was a spiritual upheaval of which Wales had never before experienced the like, and its ultimate result was the complete renewal of the Welsh people in all aspects of the national life and character. Wales was never the same after this remarkable visitation from on high during the eighteenth century.

When Howell Harris began his mission in North Wales in 1738, three leaders of Welsh Methodism had emerged, *viz.* Harris himself, Daniel Rowland of Llangeitho, and Howell Davies, who became the Apostle of Pembrokeshire. These men were soon joined by others, *viz.* William Williams of Pantycelyn, who was converted when he was a student at Llwyn-llwyd Academy, under Harris's ministry; and John Powell, the rector of Llanmartin and Wilcrick, Monmouthshire. William Williams became the hymnologist of the movement as Charles Wesley in England; and his hymns are still sung by the Welsh people on all occasions. These men, together with certain lay exhorters, formed themselves into an Association in 1742, and began to organise the movement which ultimately influenced all phases of Welsh religious life, and created as its permanent body the

Calvinistic Methodist, or Presbyterian Church of Wales.

Harris met George Whitefield in 1739, and the two men—of kindred mind and spirit—began to co-operate in the work of spreading the religious revival which was then beginning to be felt in England too. They were both Calvinists in theological outlook, and Harris sided with Whitefield when the latter broke with John and Charles Wesley on the issue of Calvinism versus Arminianism. Whitefield presided as moderator in the famous Welsh-English Calvinistic Association at Watford near Caerphilly in 1743. The members of that association were Harris, Rowland, Williams of Pantycelyn and John Powell (representing the Welsh Methodists); and Whitefield, John Cennick and Joseph Humphreys (representing the English Calvinistic Methodists). In the course of the same year Peter Williams was converted under Whitefield's ministry, and very soon he too became one of the leaders of the new movement; his work as a Biblical commentator has made him a family name in Wales for generations.

During the next decade the work was consolidated. The societies were organised, zones arranged for public and private exhorters, superintendents were appointed, and monthly and quarterly associations were regularly held to control the work. "During the formative years in the history of Welsh Calvinistic Methodism," writes the Rev. G. T. Roberts, "its organising genius, without any doubt, was Howell Harris." He laid down the foundations of a system which has remained, in its broad outlines, to this day.

Harris, during this period, became known not only in his native land, but also in England. Whitefield brought him to London, and during the latter's visits to Scotland and America Harris was in charge of the work at Whitefield's Tabernacle in Moorfields and other centres, a task with many a heartache. Despite their doctrinal differences, Harris kept in touch with the two Wesleys, and he attended many of their Conferences; he always endeavoured to heal the breach between them and Whitefield. Harris's role was that of a peacemaker. Beneath his turbulent spirit there was a loving heart, and that heart went out in love and sympathy to all those who adhered to the evangelical faith. This, perhaps, was his greatest contribution to British Methodism. He had a vision of an evangelical movement comprising not only the conflicting Methodists, but also the Moravians; for many years he spared no time and energy in trying to give effect to that vision. He finally failed to unite the evangelical forces of the eighteenth century, but was not the effort worth while?

Bennett has referred to Harris's love for the widow, Mrs. Parry of Tal-y-llyn, who died in 1738. A few years later he became attached to another widow, Mrs. Elizabeth James of Abergavenny. She, too, it is quite evident, was fond of him, but Harris persuaded himself that she was destined to be Whitefield's wife; and after a hard struggle he gave her up in favour of his friend, who married her at Caerphilly in November 1741. His thoughts then turned to one of his converts, Miss Anne Williams, daughter of John Williams of Skreen, both of whom are referred to by Bennett. Her family were bitterly opposed to the match, but after a long and stormy courtship they were married at Ystrad-ffin in June 1744; and Harris brought his bride to live in his mother's cottage at Trevecka. Three children were born of the marriage, but only one of them survived infancy, viz. Elizabeth, who in the course of time became the wife of Charles Prichard, a surgeon, of Brecon.

Harris, in the 1740's, came under the influence of the Moravians, and to some extent accepted some of their theological views. He began to preach their "blood and wounds" theology, and before long he began to lay a peculiar emphasis on the Person of Christ, proclaiming that God had suffered and that God Himself had died upon Calvary. In short, in his emphasis on the Godhead of Christ, he had drifted into the old Patripassian heresy. His Welsh brethren, of course, remonstrated with him, and Daniel Rowland, in 1750, published a pamphlet against him, entitled *A Conversation between an Orthodox Methodist and a Mistaken One.*

In the meantime, Harris had become very intolerant, and would brook no interference, and would accept no advice from his friends and followers. He suffered from bouts of passion, and became quite unmanageable. He separated from Rowland and the other leaders, and for a time he roamed to and fro, rallying his supporters and setting up an independent Association. The Welsh Methodists were rent in twain, and wholly disrupted, "Rowland's People" and "Harris's People" meeting apart. Eventually Harris's friends denied him, one by one, and he was left almost alone. The societies were neglected, and many converts grew cold and fell into a backslidden condition. It was "a time of troubles"—to use Professor Arnold Toynbee's phrase—with the Welsh Methodists, and the whole movement was in grievous danger.

That was the situation in 1750, when Harris separated from his brethren. He retired to Trevecka, and gave up itinerating. He thought that his work was all over, and in a manner of speaking it was. Over twenty years of life were still in store for him, but the accomplishments of those years were as nothing compared with what he did during those wonderful years, 1735-50. The peaceful surroundings of Trevecka soon helped him to regain his health and balance, and soon he was fully employed once again. He was given the opportunity of fulfilling an old dream. He had read of Professor Franke's Pietistic Institution in Halle, Germany, and now—at Trevecka—he determined to found a religious community, where his followers could live, work and worship together. He pulled down his home, and began to build an edifice large enough to house the "Family," as it came to be known. Members of the Family placed all their possessions at the disposal of the community, and some of them gave large sums of money. In a few years' time the Family consisted of over a hundred people, and a variety of trades and crafts were practised there. Farms in the locality were rented and occupied by members of the Family. Harris became interested in agriculture and rural crafts, and together with others he had a hand in founding the Breconshire Agricultural Society—the first society of its kind in Wales.

The country at that time was at war with France, and this was regarded in many religious circles as a struggle between Protestantism and Roman Catholicism. Early in 1756 five young men of the Family joined the 58th Regiment—three of them eventually fought at Quebec under General Wolfe. In 1759 Harris himself formed a company of men, and was offered the position of an Ensign in the Breconshire Militia. Later he was promoted to the rank of Captain. He joined the Militia on condition that he would be allowed to preach in all places wherever he went. During this period (1759-62), he and his militia-men are found in such places as Torrington, Bideford, Bridgwater, Plymouth, Great Yarmouth, etc., and many stories are told of his evangelistic work in these and in other places.

In 1762 the Militia was disbanded and Harris resigned his commission. By now the old animosities were subsiding, and Harris was invited by his old friends to return to his former place in the Methodist movement. A new spirit of revival was in the land, and fanned by the hymns of Williams of Pantycelyn and Daniel Rowland's ministry at Llangeitho, the fire spread abroad. Harris could not resist this call, and in 1763 he rejoined his old comrades. Once again he set out on his preaching tours, revisiting the old preaching-stations, and huge crowds followed him everywhere. But his powers were waning, and he felt at times that there was an air of suspicion in some quarters; many exhorters would not have him to rule over them. But he was given a warm welcome by the common people, and tears of joy were shed by his old converts when they saw his face and heard his voice again.

The Family was still flourishing at Trevecka, and Harris was fortunate in having men like Evan Moses, Evan Roberts, William Roberts, and James Prichard to take charge of the business affairs of the community. In 1768, Lady Huntingdon opened a college for her preachers at Trevecka. The godly John Fletcher of Madeley was appointed President of the new college, but during his absence Harris exercised some measure of spiritual oversight over the young students. He met with some difficulties during this period, but on the whole it was a happy time and he enjoyed the company of his brethren, especially during the College Anniversaries.

His life was now drawing to its close. In 1770, his old friends Howell Davies and George Whitefield died: during the same year he lost his wife. He himself, too, was sickening, and after a few years of intermittent suffering he was released. He died on 21 July 1773, and his mortal remains were buried within the walls of Talgarth church, near the Communion Table where he had found Christ at the beginning of his ministry. The inscription on his memorial reads thus:

Near the Communion Table lie the remains of Howell Harris, Esquire; born at Trevecka, January 23rd, 1714. Here, where his body lies, he was convinced of sin, had his pardon sealed, felt the power of Christ's precious blood at the Holy Communion. Having tasted grace himself, he resolved to declare to others what God had done for his soul. He was the first itinerant Preacher of Redemption in this period of Revival in England and Wales. He preached the Gospel for the space of thirty-nine years, till he was taken to his final Rest. He received those who sought Salvation into his house. Then sprang up the Family at Trevecka, to whom he faithfully ministered unto his end, as an indefatigable servant of God and a faithful member of the Church of England. His end was more blessed than his beginning. Looking to Jesus crucified, he rejoiced to the last that death had lost its sting. He fell asleep in Jesus at Trevecka, July 21st, 1773, and now rests blessedly from all his labours.

Howell Harris has been justly regarded as the foremost Welshman of his age. Sir Owen M. Edwards wrote of him: "Whatever else can be said of Harris's oratory and genius and of his strange projects, the awakening of Wales from a sleep that was paralysing its national vigour can be attributed to him more than to anybody else." Dr. R. T. Jenkins, an eminent Welsh historian and our authority on eighteenth-century Wales, wrote of him: "It is difficult to believe that Howell Harris was not the greatest Welshman of his century." His latest biographer, the Rev. Griffith T. Roberts, has this to say of him: "This powerful revivalist, able organiser, and great Methodist was God's gift to Wales, and very few men have so deeply and so permanently influenced the religious life of the Principality as Howell Harris."

After his death the work of the revival went on successfully; the gains were consolidated, and chapels were built everywhere. Some trouble arose before the end

of the century owing to the Sabellian principles held by
Peter Williams, one of the leaders. Eventually he was
expelled for his views, after bitter controversy. Daniel
Rowland died in 1790; William Williams in 1791; and
Peter Williams in 1796. New leaders arose, such as
David Jones of Llan-gan and Thomas Charles of Bala;
and lay preachers of the calibre of Ebenezer Richard and
Ebenezer Morris in South Wales, and Thomas Jones of
Denbigh and John Elias of Anglesey, confirmed the
Methodist societies in the evangelical faith. In 1811—a
fateful year in the history of Welsh Methodism—some
lay preachers were ordained by the Association in North
and South Wales, and by this act the Methodists finally
separated themselves from the Established Church and
became known as the Calvinistic Methodist Connexion.

APPENDIX[1]

Mr. Evans admits that Howell Harris was honest enough to write the harshest truth concerning himself, but yet he holds that he was guilty, not only of "inaccuracy" but of "falsity"; that is, that he was given to bearing false witness. Harris wrote very much—more, perhaps, than the reader can ever imagine. He gives an account of vicissitudes of his career time and again during the course of the years, and that in a free, open way, from memory, when he had nothing else at hand to rely upon. It would not surprise us if so busy a man and so prolific a writer should be guilty of an occasional inconsistency—apparent at any rate. Sometimes the story of one year runs into that of another year, and a few incidents are incorrectly dated. Such things are seen in works more sacred than his. The wonder is that he is so accurate, when all the circumstances are taken into consideration. It may be admitted that one may have the impression of "falsity" with regard to the story, but who is responsible for this? For instance, Mr. Evans tells us three things in connection with the matter under consideration:

1. That Harris was educated in Vavasor Griffiths's school.
2. That his teacher subsequently became his unsuccessful rival in courtship.
3. That he went from that school to Oxford.

These propositions are based on the Diaries. On the same basis exactly we say:

1. That Harris never attended Vavasor Griffiths's school.
2. That Vavasor Griffiths had died many months before the commencement of Harris's courtship with Anne Williams of Skreen.
3. That Harris went to Oxford from his school—mastering at Llangasty, a full four years after leaving Llwyn-llwyd.

If the original manuscript of the Autobiography were available it could quite likely be easily established that its editor was no more accurate a reader than the author of *The Reformers of Wales*.

In saying this we would not excuse Methodist historians for repeating errors, time and again. They should certainly have paid more attention to the material at their disposal. It is difficult to understand the indifference of the Calvinistic Methodist

---

[1] See footnote on page 40.

Connexion to its early history. No denomination in Wales has better material at hand, and no denomination has so failed to appreciate the value of such material. It is hoped that the increasing interest shown in recent Associations will bring forth an undertaking worthy of the Connexion.[1]

In this unfinished list of Howell Harris's "most obvious defects," Mr. Evans places first his lack of education; and right out of the blue he speaks favourably of the Bishop of Llandaff, who refused to license such an uneducated man. It is not known whether his Lordship ever had the opportunity of refusing, but it is known that one of his predecessors deprived Walter Cradoc of his licence, calling him "a bold, ignorant fellow," and sending examples of his low style to the Archbishop of Canterbury. Are we to gather from this, together with the fact that Cradoc's name is not found in the University Registers, that he too was a man of no learning? No, certainly not. Episcopal care for the fitness of the clergy kept out the Methodist, but something else cast out the Nonconformist.[2] Let all the Bishops of Llandaff say what they will, Nonconformist ministers from the beginning were men of deep, wide and disciplined learning. Who will dare to query this when we remember that Matthew Henry could be regarded as an example of the average among them? Only one out of seven of them, it is true, is noted as a "scholar" in Dr. Evans's list,[3] but it is likely that this number had some mystical quality for him. But as *they* were characterised by scholarship, Mr. Evans would have us understand, on the other hand, that ignorance was the special characteristic of the Methodist! After emphasising the above "defect," Mr. Evans goes on to say that *more* education would have caused Harris to develop into an ecclesiastical dignitary, with no connection at all with Methodism. This would have been worse than the former; but Providence knew her task perfectly—as far as education was con-

[1] After these words were written, the Calvinistic Methodist Historical Society was founded, of which Mr. Bennett was a leading member for many years. This Society, during the last forty years or so, has done much to modify the author's strictures.—G. M. R.

[2] The Methodists, in the eighteenth century, regarded themselves as members of the Church of England in spite of the irregularity of their position within the Church. The Nonconformists of those days were the children of the older Puritan movement, *viz.*, the Independents, Baptists, Presbyterians and the Quakers, especially the first two.—G. M. R.

[3] Dr. John Evans (c. 1680-1730), the Presbyterian divine, compiled "lists" dealing with Nonconformity between the years 1717 and 1729. These "lists" have been the subject of much controversy with Welsh historians.—G. M. R.

cerned! Very little education was needful at that time to produce
a "dignitary,"[1] but even that—such as it was—could very well
spoil a good Methodist; and Welsh Methodists ought to be
thankful to that Providence that kept Harris far enough from
Oxford! Mr. Evans has not troubled to show why that which
was the native atmosphere of English Methodism should prove
to be so deadly to Welsh Methodism; and he has chosen to dis-
regard the fact that certain good people who placed great importance on learning urged the Bishop's rejected candidate to
seek orders with them!

But setting jesting aside, must we regard Howell Harris, like
the Apostles of old, as unlettered and unlearned, when assessed
according to the standard of learning common among public
men of his age and country? We do not know. It is true that
he did not spend any time at University, but that is true of the
majority of Welsh reformers—of Griffith Jones and Daniel Rowland; of Enoch Francis, the greatest light among the Baptists;
and of David Davies of Swansea, who was as much a "Father"
to Independency as was his contemporary, Thomas Charles, to
Methodism. It is true that Harris himself was conscious of his
ignorance, and was desirous of improving himself; but is this a
characteristic of Methodism only? We may readily grant that
Mr. B. G. Evans can see certain evidences of a lack of culture
in his writings: but it is also true that the *"wooden spoons"* of
today can challenge the *senior wranglers* of the reign of
George II.[2] Mr. Evans states that Harris's friends and fellow-
labourers were as conscious as he was of his educational defects,
and, in proof of this, he refers to a letter written by Miles Harry[3]
to him trying to persuade him *not* to go to complete his studies—
a pretty strong proof, one would think, that the Methodist's
ignorance did not greatly offend the Baptist's susceptibility.
"Though by applying yourself to study," he says, "you might be
able to speak more accurately, yet, I believe, not more efficaci-
ously." Whether this sentence indicates that he regarded Harris
as a more than usually uncouth speaker, let the reader decide.

One thing is evident: Harris, from the beginning, was a very
"effective" speaker. If we have to admit that some of his contemporaries had a sharper edge to their weapons, it must be admitted also that there was much greater power in his stroke,
otherwise he would not have laboured more abundantly than
they all, under such a disadvantage. As a rule, the effectual

---

[1] See Wesley's *Works*, viii., p. 219.

[2] *Cf.* Macaulay's *Essay on the War of the Succession in Spain.*

[3] A well-known Baptist minister, of Monmouthshire, who was
friendly with Harris at the beginning of his preaching career.—
G. M. R.

speaker is the most powerful influence in the land. The people will go out to the wilderness to listen to him, in spite of what the Sanhedrin may say. Rather than accept a ruling that so-and-so is a Grecian and so-and-so is a Barbarian, the people will judge their teachers according to the quality of the feast they have prepared. While Dr. Walker[1] and his kind laboured to show the Nonconformists as uncultured cobblers, etc., the common people took little notice of them, instead they sang drolly:

> "Tom Parry, without surplice, the people do say,
> Is a far better preacher than the Parson of Hay;
> The cobblers and tailors and weavers—'tis odd!
> Can beat Oxford scholars, and lead men to God."[2]

Similarly, a generation or two later, the early Methodists could "beat the great scholars of Oxford" and of Carmarthen too. In spite of all endeavours of Dr. Walker's imitators to despise the one and to over-exalt the other, the letters written by the Nonconformists themselves, plainly show that the ignorant Methodist was "better at preaching" than anybody who had laboured in the field before him.

If the Methodists are to be forbidden to imitate other denominations by referring to their Fathers as men of deep and wide learning, all is well. That was not the secret of their power, and they never claimed it. Very often we find Howell Harris, in reverent wonder, astonished at the success which followed his endeavours, being in his own estimation such a worthless nonentity; while many abler men had laboured throughout the years "without catching anything." Probably there was need of qualifications more indispensable even than learning, to deal with the task which had to be done in Wales in those days. Gamaliel did not originate any moral revival in spite of the great demand for it. Erasmus and Buchanan were better scholars than Martin Luther and John Knox; but the latter had the power of conviction which could move the mountains which the power of the former's learning could not budge. And whatever is said of Howell Harris, he too possessed the power of conviction and indomitable zeal which caused his heart to be warmed within him. A fire was kindled, and he spoke with such effect that, in the words of Joshua Thomas,[3] "there was a great revival in a drowsy generation." And before long we see the best type of

---

[1] Dr. Walker, author of *The Sufferings of the Clergy*.—G. M. R.

[2] The Welsh skit was composed by a Mr. Price—brother to the Rev. Joseph Price—of the Shephouse, near Hay.—G. M. R.

[3] The Welsh Baptist historian who published a remarkable history of the Welsh Baptists in 1778.—G. M. R.

scholars admitting in a very practical way that the young man "of uncultured mind" possessed something far more valuable than learning to give to his country. We find them imploring him, and fervently pleading with him, time and again, to visit their localities, and receiving him amongst themselves as the angel of God, and blessing the Almighty for sending him.

BIBLIOGRAPHY

The list below is confined to works available in English. Many of them are out of print, of course, but they can be consulted in libraries. Whilst the bibliography cannot claim to be exhaustive, an attempt has been made to be as comprehensive as possible. The bibliography relates to the whole of Harris's life, and has not been confined to the earlier period which is the subject of Bennett's book. A number of works on both the religious and secular background to his activities and on the history of his home, Trefeca, have also been included.

Evangelical Library of Wales   E. WYN JAMES

(a) BOOKS (arranged chronologically):

1. Howell Harris, *The Last Message, and Dying Testimony, of Howell Harris, Esqr* (Trefeca, 1774).

2. Benjamin La Trobe (ed.), *A Brief Account of the Life of Howell Harris, Esq.; Extracted from Papers Written by Himself* (Trefeca, 1791). New edition: *Howell Harris: His Own Story* (Chepstow, 1984).

3. John Bulmer, *Memoirs of the Life and Religious Labours of Howell Harris, Esq.* (Haverfordwest, 1824).

4. [A. C. H. Seymour], *The Life and Times of Selina Countess of Huntingdon*, 2 vols (London, 1839) — an index to these volumes was published as a supplement to vol. 5 of the *Wesley Historical Society Proceedings*.

5. Edward Morgan, *The Life and Times of Howel Harris, Esq.* (Holywell, 1852).

6. Helen C. Knight, *Lady Huntingdon and Her Friends* (New York, 1853; republished in 1979 by Baker Book House, Grand Rapids, Michigan).

7. Alfred H. New, *The Coronet and the Crown: or, Memorials of . . . Selina, Countess of Huntingdon* (London, 1857).

8. Thomas Rees, *History of Protestant Nonconformity in Wales* (London, 1861; enlarged ed. 1883).

9. William Williams, *Welsh Calvinistic Methodism: A Historical Sketch* (London, 1872; enlarged ed. 1884).

10. Hugh J. Hughes, *Life of Howell Harris, the Welsh Reformer* (London & Newport, 1892).

11. David Young, *The Origin and History of [Wesleyan] Methodism in Wales and the Borders* (London, 1893).

12. William Evans, *An Outline of the History of Welsh Theology* (London & Newport, 1900).

13. David Jones, *Life and Times of Griffith Jones* (London & Bangor, 1902).

14. H. Elvet Lewis, *Nonconformity in Wales* (London, 1904).

15. Edward Griffiths, *The Presbyterian Church of Wales (Calvinistic Methodists) Historical Hand-book, 1735-1905* (Wrexham, 1905).

16. Joseph Evans, *Biographical Dictionary of Ministers and Preachers of the Welsh Calvinistic Methodist Body* (Caernarfon, 1907).

17. D. E. Jenkins, *Calvinistic Methodist Holy Orders* (Caernarfon, 1911).

18. H. Elvet Lewis, *Howell Harris and the Welsh Revivalists* (London, 1911).

19. John Davies, *Howell Harris* (Aberafan, 1912).

20. M. H. Jones, *Bethlehem C.M. Church, Talgarth: A History of Calvinistic Methodism in Talgarth, 1743-1923* (Talgarth, 1924).

21. J. M. Witherow, *Church Rebels and Pioneers* (London, 1928).

22. Owen M. Edwards, *Homes of Wales,* trans. T. Eurfyl Jones (Wrexham, 1931), pp. 92-102.

23. M. H. Jones, *The Trevecka Letters* (Caernarfon, 1932).

24. John Roberts, *The Calvinistic Methodism of Wales* (Caernarfon, 1934).

25. Mabel Bickerstaff, *Our Children's Heritage: Being a Short History of the Calvinistic Methodists Told for Children* (Caernarfon, 1934).

26. D. E. Jenkins (ed.), *Religious Societies (Dr. Woodward's "Account")* (Liverpool, 1935).

27. M. Watcyn-Williams, *Creative Fellowship: An Outline of the History of Calvinistic Methodism in Wales* (Caernarfon, 1935).

28. A. H. Williams, *Welsh Wesleyan Methodism, 1800-1858* (Bangor, 1935).

29. M. G. Jones, *The Charity School Movement* (Cambridge, 1938).

30. R. T. Jenkins, 'Methodism and Associated Movements', in *A History of Carmarthenshire,* ed. J.E. Lloyd, vol. II (Cardiff, 1939).

31. W. P. Jones, *Trevecca College, 1842-1942* (Trefeca, 1942).

32. Thomas Kelly, *Griffith Jones, Llanddowror: Pioneer in Adult Education* (Cardiff, 1950).

33. David Williams, *A History of Modern Wales* (London, 1950; revised ed. 1977).

34. Griffith T. Roberts, *Howell Harris* (London, 1951).

35. Gomer M. Roberts (ed.), *Selected Trevecka Letters (1742-1747)* (Caernarfon, 1956); *Selected Trevecka Letters (1747-1794)* (Caernarfon, 1962).

36. Tom Beynon, *Howell Harris, Reformer and Soldier (1714-1773)* (Caernarfon, 1958).

37. Mabel Bickerstaff, *There Was a Man Sent . . . : An Outline of the Story of Howell Harris* (Trefeca, 1959).

38. J. E. Lloyd & R. T. Jenkins (eds), *The Dictionary of Welsh Biography down to 1940* (London, 1959).

39. Tom Beynon, *Howell Harris's Visits to London* (Aberystwyth, 1960).

40. Eifion Evans, *Revivals: Their Rise, Progress and Achievements* (London, 1960; new ed. Bridgend, 1986).

41. R. R. Williams, *Flames from the Altar: Howell Harris and His Contemporaries* (Caernarfon, 1962).

42. Geoffrey F. Nuttall, *Howel Harris, 1714-1773: The Last Enthusiast* (Cardiff, 1965).

43. Tom Beynon, *Howell Harris's Visits to Pembrokeshire* (Aberystwyth, 1966).

44. Geoffrey F. Nuttall, *The Significance of Trevecca College, 1768-91* (London, 1968).

45. J. Gwilym Jones, *William Williams, Pantycelyn* (Cardiff, 1969).

46. Arnold A. Dallimore, *George Whitefield,* vol. I (London, 1970); vol. II (Edinburgh, 1980).

47. A. H. Williams (ed.), *John Wesley in Wales, 1739-1790* (Cardiff, 1971).

48. Leighton H. James, *Howell Harris: The Eighteenth Century Exhorter* (London, 1972).

49. Gilbert W. Kirby, *The Elect Lady* (Croydon, 1972).

50. William Williams, Pantycelyn, *The Experience Meeting,* trans. Bethan Lloyd-Jones (Bridgend, 1973).

51. Eifion Evans, *Howel Harris, Evangelist (1714-1773)* (Cardiff, 1974).

52. Owain W. Jones & David Walker (eds), *Links with the Past: Swansea & Brecon [Diocese] Historical Essays* (Llandybïe, 1974).

53. D. Martyn Lloyd-Jones, *Romans: An Exposition of Chapter 8:5-17 — The Sons of God* (Edinburgh, 1974), pp. 316, 348-9.

54. Gomer M. Roberts, 'Calvinistic Methodism in Glamorgan, 1737-1773', in *Glamorgan County History,* vol. IV, ed. Glanmor Williams (Cardiff, 1974).

55. Edwin Welch (ed.), *Two Calvinistic Methodist Chapels, 1743-1811: The London Tabernacle and Spa Fields Chapel* (London, 1975).

56. Geraint H. Jenkins, *Literature, Religion and Society in Wales, 1660-1730* (Cardiff, 1978).

57. Emyr Roberts & R. Geraint Gruffydd, *Revival and Its Fruit* (Bridgend, 1981).

58. Glyn Tegai Hughes, *Williams Pantycelyn* (Cardiff, 1983).

59. Gareth Elwyn Jones, *Modern Wales: A Concise History, c.1485-1979*

(Cambridge, 1984).

60.   Eifion Evans, *Daniel Rowland and the Great Evangelical Awakening in Wales* (Edinburgh, 1985).

61.   Roger L. Brown, *The Welsh Evangelicals* (Tongwynlais, 1986).

62.   Meic Stephens (ed.), *The Oxford Companion to the Literature of Wales* (Oxford, 1986).

(b) PERIODICALS:

This list is confined to articles published in the twentieth century. Periodicals are listed alphabetically, articles are listed chronologically under each periodical.

1.   *Anglo-Welsh Review*
      Gareth Davies, 'Trevecka — Is This the End?', vol. 15, no. 35 (1965).

2.   *Banner of Truth*
      Iain H. Murray, 'The Great Awakening in Wales', 2 (Feb. 1956).

      S. M. Houghton, 'George Whitefield and Welsh Methodism', 51 (Nov./Dec. 1967) — an abridgement of an article published in the *Evangelical Quarterly,* vol. 22 (1950).

      Geoffrey Thomas, 'Trevecca College and the Countess of Huntingdon', 61 (Oct. 1968).

      John Owen, 'A Memoir of Daniel Rowlands of Llangeitho', 215-16 (Aug./Sept. 1981) — a reprint of a biography of Rowland published in 1848.

      An index to issues 1-263 (Sept. 1955-August 1985) of the *Banner of Truth,* compiled by E. M. Keen, has been published by the Banner of Truth Trust, 3 Murrayfield Road, Edinburgh EH12 6EL, Scotland.

3.   *Bathafarn* (Journal of the Historical Society of the [Wesleyan] Methodist Church in Wales)

      Tom Beynon, 'Extracts from the Diaries of Howell Harris', vols 4 (1949), 6 (1951), 9 (1954) and 10 (1955).

      Griffith T. Roberts, 'John Wesley Visits Wales', vol. 13 (1958).

      A. H. Williams, 'The Leaders of English and Welsh Methodism, 1738-91', vols 16 (1961), 17 (1962), 21 (1966)-24 (1969).

      A. H. Williams, 'John Wesley's Visits to Builth, 1743-1750', vol. 20 (1965).

      An index to vols 1 (1946)-20 (1965) is to be found in vol. 21 (1966).

4.   *Brycheiniog* (Transactions of the Brecknock Society)
      Gomer M. Roberts, 'Letter of Howell Harris, Trevecka, to Penry Williams, Pen-pont', vol. 2 (1956).

Gomer M. Roberts, 'Gleanings from the Trevecka Letters', vols 2 (1956) and 3 (1957).

John Davies, 'Howell Harris and the Trevecka Settlement', vol. 9 (1963).

Gareth Davies, 'Trevecka (1706-1964)', vol. 15 (1971).

5. *Church History*
    Richard W. Evans, 'The Relations of George Whitefield and Howell Harris', vol. 30:2 (June, 1961).

6. *Country Life*
    G. Edwards, 'An Early Land Settlement', 7 May 1938.

7. *Y Cymmrodor* (Magazine of the Honourable Society of Cymmrodorion)
    R. T. Jenkins, *The Moravian Brethren in North Wales,* vol. 45 (London, 1938).

8. *Evangelical Library Bulletin*
    David Boorman, 'Spiritual Forerunners of Daniel Rowland', 22 (Spring 1959).

    Elizabeth Braund, 'Before the Dawn', 27 (Autumn 1961).

    Elizabeth Braund, 'The Day of His Power', 28 (Spring 1962).

    Eliseus Howells, 'Howell Harris', 40 (Spring 1968).

    Eifion Evans, 'William Williams of Pantycelyn', 42 (Spring 1969) — reprinted in *The Evangelical Magazine of Wales,* vol. 22 (1983).

    Eifion Evans, 'George Whitefield and Wales', 45 (Autumn 1970).

    Eifion Evans, 'The Confession of Faith of the Welsh Calvinistic Methodists', 51 (Winter 1973).

    An index to nos 1-70 (1945-83) of the Bulletin has been compiled and is available from the Evangelical Library, 78a Chiltern Street, London W1M 2HB, England.

9. *Evangelical Magazine of Wales*
    David Boorman, 'Howell Harris', vol. 1:5 (Summer 1956).

    Elizabeth Braund, 'The Religious Societies', vol. 1:21 (July/August 1961).

    Eifion Evans, 'Diaries Which Helped Me', vol. 1:23 (Nov./Dec. 1961).

    Elizabeth Braund, 'George Whitefield and the Religious Societies', vol. 1:24 (Jan./Feb. 1962).

    Elizabeth Braund, 'The Heart of the Matter', vol. 1:25 (March/April 1962).

    Hywel R. Jones, 'Daniel Rowland: Man of Truth and Power', vol. 10:6 (Dec. 1971/Jan. 1972)-11:2 (April/May 1972). This lecture, the Annual Lecture of the Evangelical Library of Wales for 1971, was then published in booklet form in 1972, and has subsequently been reprinted in *Gospel Tidings,* vol. 10:5 (Oct. 1986).

'Howel Harris Commemorative Issue', vol. 12:4 (Aug./Sept. 1973).

David Boorman, 'The Morning Star of the Methodist Revival: Griffith Jones of Llanddowror', vol. 21:4 (Aug./Sept. 1982).

Matthew Francis, 'Lady Huntingdon, Wales and Welshmen', vol. 21:5 (Oct./Nov. 1982) and 21:6 (Dec. 1982/Jan. 1983).

David Boorman, 'Howel Harris', vol. 22:1 (Feb./March 1983).

David Boorman, 'Daniel Rowland', vol. 22:2 (April/May 1983).

An index to this periodical is currently in preparation and will be available from the Evangelical Movement of Wales, Bryntirion, Bridgend, Mid Glamorgan CF31 4DX, Wales.

10. *The Gospel Magazine*
Eifion Evans, 'David Jones of Llangan', April 1967.

11. *Gower* (Journal of the Gower Society)
Gomer M. Roberts, 'Early Methodism in Gower', vol. 10 (1957).

12. *Journal of the Historical Society of the Presbyterian Church of Wales,* vols 1-60 (1916-76); new series, vol. 1 (1977) to date.

This journal contains articles too numerous to mention on various aspects of the life of Howell Harris, together with many extracts from his diaries and copies of his letters. In the course of the years, two twelve-part series of 'Trevecka MSS. Supplements' to this journal have been published containing transcripts of many of the 'Trevecka Letters' and some extracts from Harris's diaries, together with another supplement in three parts of 'The Itinerary of Howell Harris' (1735-73). The issues of the journal for March 1936 and December 1964 between them include an index to the contents from May 1916 to September 1964.

13. *Journal of the Welsh Bibliographical Society*
M. H. Jones, 'The Trevecka MSS. and Library', vol. 1:1 (June 1910).

M. H. Jones, 'Joseph Harris', vol. 3:6 (July 1929).

14. *Journal of Welsh Ecclesiastical History*
A. H. Williams, 'Daniel Rowland and the Great Evangelical Awakening in Wales', vol. 2 (1985).

15. *The Library*
John Ballinger, 'The Trevecca Press', vol. 6 (1905) — cf. Ifano Jones, *A History of Printing and Printers in Wales* (Cardiff, 1925), chapter 11.

16. *Montgomeryshire Collections* (Transactions of the Powysland Club)
Gomer M. Roberts, 'The Early Methodist Societies in Montgomeryshire', vol. 59 (1965-6).

Gomer M. Roberts, 'Howel Harris and Montgomeryshire', vol. 63:1 (1973).

An index to the Transactions for 1868-1956 was published by the Club in 1962.

17. *Ours: A Christian Youth Magazine* (published by the Evangelical Movement of Wales)

David Boorman, 'Howell Harris — The Early Years', March/April 1966.

David Boorman, 'Howell Harris — Evangelist and Teacher', Summer 1966.

18. *Puritan and Westminster Conference Papers*
Eifion Evans, 'Daniel Rowland' in *Profitable for Doctrine and Reproof* (1967).

D. Martyn Lloyd-Jones, 'William Williams and Welsh Calvinistic Methodism' in *The Manifold Grace of God* (1968).

Eifion Evans, 'Adding to the Church — In the Teaching of the Welsh Calvinistic Methodists' in *Adding to the Church* (1973).

D. Martyn Lloyd-Jones, 'Howell Harris and Revival' in *Adding to the Church* (1973).

An index by E. M. Keen to the twenty printed volumes of reports from 1958 to 1978 is to be found in *Light from John Bunyan and Other Puritans*, the report of the papers read at the 1978 Westminster Conference. The Banner of Truth Trust have gathered together Dr Lloyd-Jones's annual addresses to these conferences between 1959 and 1978 in a volume entitled *The Puritans: Their Origins and Successors* (Edinburgh, 1987).

19. *Studies in Church History* [Transactions of the Ecclesiastical History Society]
R. Buick Knox, 'The Wesleys and Howell Harris', vol. 3, ed. G. J. Cuming (1966).

20. *Transactions of the Carmarthenshire Antiquarian Society*
M. H. Jones, 'The Rise and Growth of Methodism in Carmarthenshire', vols 2 (1906-7) and 3 (1907-8).

M. H. Jones, 'Howell Harris and Griffith Jones, Llanddowror', vol. 10 (1914-15).

M. H. Jones, 'An Eighteenth Century Pocket Book of the Roads and Post Towns in England & Wales', vol. 17 (1923-4).

M. H. Jones, 'Carmarthenshire Hymnists', vol. 21 (1927-9).

An index to the Transactions for 1905-77, compiled by A. M. W. Green, was published by the Society in 1981.

21. *Transactions of the Honourable Society of Cymmrodorion*
M. H. Jones, 'Howell Harris, Citizen and Patriot', Session 1908-9.

Geoffrey F. Nuttall, 'The Students of Trevecca College, 1768-1791', Session 1967, part 2.

22. *Transactions of the Radnorshire Society*
Tom Beynon, 'Howell Harris accused of riotous assault at Presteigne and Knighton Quarter Sessions', vol. 20 (1950).

An index to the Transactions for 1956-80 was published by the Society in 1984 and for 1981-5 in 1987.

23. *The Treasury* [The English-language organ of the Presbyterian Church of Wales]

    M. H. Jones, 'The First Welsh Methodist Religious Society', vol. 10 (1909)

    J. Morgan Jones, 'Howell Harris', vol. 2 (1914).

    Howell Harris Hughes, 'Howell Harris', vol. 2 (1914).

    Abraham Morris, 'Welsh Presbyterianism', vols 13 (1925) and 14 (1926).

    John Roberts, 'The Calvinistic Methodism of Wales', vols 21 (1933) and 22 (1934) — also published in book form in 1934.

    H. P. Roberts, 'The Methodist Fathers', vol. 23 (1935).

    'Howell Harris in Denbighshire', vol. 23 (1935).

    Tom Beynon, 'Howell Harris at Llandrindod', vol. 23 (1949).

    A. Victor Murray, 'Cheshunt and Trevecca', vol. 24 (1950).

    Gomer M. Roberts, 'Howell Harris', vol. 97 (1973).

    Olwen Lloyd Jones, 'The Story of Our Church: II. Howel Harris of Trefeca', vol. 103 (1979).

    R. G. Davies, 'Trefeca and Great Yarmouth: Further Thoughts on the Howell Harris 1760 Link', vol. 9 (1985).

24. *Wesley Historical Society Proceedings*
    This publication contains a number of articles relating to Howell Harris and Methodism in Wales in the eighteenth century. An index to vols 1-30 (1897-1956), compiled by John A. Vickers, was published by the Society in 1960.

(c) MANUSCRIPTS:

The archives of the Presbyterian Church of Wales, a substantial collection which includes Harris's numerous letters and diaries, is deposited at the National Library of Wales at Aberystwyth, where its schedules may be consulted. (See Gildas Tibbott & K. Monica Davies, 'The Archives of the Calvinistic Methodist or Presbyterian Church of Wales', *Journal of the National Library of Wales,* vol. 5:1, Summer 1947.)

The National Library's own collection of manuscripts, and other collections deposited there, also contain many items relevant to Harris and Welsh Calvinistic Methodism. Four volumes of the Library's *Handlist of Manuscripts* have been published to date.

Special mention should also perhaps be made of the archives of the Cheshunt Foundation at Westminster College, Cambridge, a foundation which is a continuation of the college founded by the Countess of Huntingdon at Trefeca in 1768.

A small museum is housed in the vestry of the Memorial Chapel at Trefeca.

(d) BIBLIOGRAPHIES:

Board of Celtic Studies of the University of Wales, *A Bibliography of the History of Wales*, second ed. (Cardiff 1962); supplements in *The Bulletin of the Board of Celtic Studies*, 1963, 1966, 1969 and 1972.

Alun Eirug Davies, *Welsh Language and Welsh Dissertations Accepted by British, American and German Universities, 1887-1971* (Cardiff, 1973); supplements in each issue of *Studia Celtica* from vol. 10/11 (1975-6).

H. Turner Evans, *A Bibliography of Welsh Hymnology to 1960* (Welsh Library Association, 1977).

Meic Stephens (ed.), *A Reader's Guide to Wales* (London, 1973).

For Welsh-language materials on Harris and Welsh Calvinistic Methodism one should also refer to Thomas Parry & Merfyn Morgan, *Llyfryddiaeth Llenyddiaeth Gymraeg* (Cardiff, 1976; supplement in *The Bulletin of the Board of Celtic Studies*, 1982), D. Ben Rees, *Haneswyr yr Hen Gorff* (Liverpool & Llanddewibrefi, 1981), and the bibliographies compiled by K. Monica Davies in the two-volume history of Welsh Calvinistic Methodism from 1735 to 1814 edited by Gomer M. Roberts, *Hanes Methodistiaeth Galfinaidd Cymru* (Caernarfon, 1973 & 1978).

Bibliographies of the publications of the three longest-serving editors of the *Journal of the Historical Society of the Presbyterian Church of Wales*, and all prolific writers on Harris, have been compiled:

> for M. H. Jones in his posthumous volume, *The Trevecka Letters* (Caernarfon 1932);
>
> for Tom Beynon in the *Journal of the Historical Society of the Presbyterian Church of Wales*, vol. 47:2 (July 1962);
>
> for Gomer M. Roberts in J. E. Wynne Davies (ed.), *Gwanwyn Duw* (Caernarfon, 1982).

A bibliography of the writings of the prominent historian Professor R. T. Jenkins, who wrote extensively on Welsh Methodist history, is to be found in the *Journal of the Welsh Bibliographical Society*, vol. 10 (1966-71). Although their main fields of speciality are the Puritan movement and the older Nonconformity, rather than Methodism, it is worth noting in passing three other bibliographies of prominent Welsh church historians, namely those of Thomas Shankland in *Trafodion Cymdeithas Hanes Bedyddwyr Cymru* 1926 and 1928, of Thomas Richards in the *Journal of the Welsh Bibliographical Society*, vol. 9:3 (Dec. 1962), and of R. Tudur Jones in E. Stanley John (ed.), *Y Gair a'r Genedl* (Swansea, 1986).

Richard Bennett (1860-1937) was a farmer from Montgomeryshire who, with a minimum of formal education, became a leading authority on Welsh Calvinistic Methodism. He came to be regarded by prominent Welsh academics as a first-rate historian (see the article on him in the *Dictionary of Welsh Biography* by R. T. Jenkins), and in 1932 his contribution in his chosen field of study was recognised when he was awarded an honorary MA degree by the University of Wales. The volume *Cyfrol Goffa Richard Bennett* (1940), eds D.

Teifigar Davies & R. W. Jones, contains a list of his publications. On Bennett see also J. Bennett Jones, 'Richard Bennett: Hanesydd a'i Gefndir', *Journal of the Historical Society of the Presbyterian Church of Wales*, vols 52 (1967) and 53 (1968).

INDEX

199

Further titles from the Evangelical Press of Wales

Martyn Lloyd-Jones: The Man and His Books by Frederick & Elizabeth Catherwood. A fascinating personal account of 'the Doctor' by his daughter and son-in-law.

Why Does God Allow War? by D. Martyn Lloyd-Jones. Biblical teaching on how Christians should face evil and suffering.

In the Shadow of Aran by Mari Jones; foreword by D. Martyn Lloyd-Jones. Popular stories from farm life in North Wales vividly illustrating spiritual truths.

The Lord Our Shepherd by J. Douglas MacMillan. The author's first-hand experience as a shepherd makes this moving study of Psalm 23 extra special.

Christian Family Matters edited by Ian Shaw; foreword by Sir Frederick Catherwood. Clear biblical guidelines by experienced contributors on marriage, parenthood, divorce, abortion and other issues that affect family life.

Christian Hymns edited by Paul E. G. Cook and Graham Harrison. A comprehensive selection of 901 hymns; a variety of editions available, including a large-type words edition and a presentation music edition.

Christian Hymn-writers by Elsie Houghton. A collection of brief biographies of some of the great hymn-writers.

A SERIES of booklets for the earnest seeker and the new Christian by Peter Jeffery, born out of the practical needs of the author's own pastoral work:

Seeking God—for the earnest seeker after faith.

All Things New—a help for those beginning the Christian life.

Walk Worthy—guidelines for those who have just started on the Christian life.

Firm Foundations (with Owen Milton). A two-month Bible study course introducing new Christians to great chapters of the Bible.

Stand Firm—a young Christian's guide to the armour of God.